C000301028

BITCH GODDESS RE

Paris: May 1968

By John Messing

Copyright JHM 2017

TABLE OF CONTENTS

Page

In memory of Pierre Arènes

Preface

Tucson, Arizona, May 16, 2017

The events of Paris in May 1968 are revisited each decade. Most publications discuss causes and consequences; reasons for its failure, and/or lessons learned. I expect the same and more for the upcoming 50th anniversary.

This book approaches the subject differently. I lived through that time as an outsider allowed in. I have tried to present just the facts as I experienced them; I have avoided editorializing.

I took no notes. It was done from memory, which does not improve with time or age, and apparently undergoes subtle changes each time it is accessed. I apologize beforehand for any errors in chronology, names, or the like. I cross-checked my recollection with several French publications of the time, as well as Internet sources. I did my utmost to remain faithful to the events as I witnessed them, the character of the people I came to know, and the spirit of the times.

I do think that history progresses in spiral fashion, and that, given recent events in the Middle East and the US, Marxism may resurge as a revolutionary ideology. I hope the book offers a glimmer of what that felt like, up close and personal, once upon a time.

Introduction

MAY 7, 1968: PLACE DE LA CONTRESCARPE

We heard the sounds of unified chants, far away.

"Here it is. Let's go."

We joined others in the street making their way towards the sound, drawn as if by a magnet.

Closer, the chant was "Long live the Paris commune."

The people possessed a quiet dignity, drawing taller in themselves as they funneled through the streets towards a vaguely understood destiny.

Then the spell broke and there were police and crowds and sounds and fury all around. We fell in behind other marchers who were singing the Internationale, but almost immediately the crowd broke up ahead and black uniformed shielded and baton wielding police came charging at us.

"Hold your ground!" came a shout from behind, where resolute arm-in-arm students several ranks deep stood ready to take the brunt of an attack.

We were caught in between, and scattered to the sides as best we could, falling back to regroup behind the front line. The police halted and were reinforced. The two lines faced off against each other.

A loudspeaker blared: "Disband, by order of the President of the Republic. Disband at once. All who do not are breaking the law and will be treated accordingly. Disband."

"Screw you!" came a shout, and derisive laughter.

Police charged again but the crowd melted in their path and the police discovered, too late, that they were in the range of pavers that began raining down on them from their flanks. One cobblestone hit a policeman on the helmet who collapsed. A second shower of pavers began. The police retreated, supporting their fallen comrade, who miraculously could still ambulate with assistance.

The police donned gas masks and began lobbing tear gas grenades. I had brought a scarf and secured it to protect my mouth and nose. We stood our ground, but finally I could stand it no longer and retreated to get air. I was choking and coughing, for a moment unable to orient myself as to the surrounding streets, but it passed quickly. Surrounded by strangers, I turned around once again. Some held hands as we marched forward, resolute, wills locked more firmly than limbs, marching for our side, come what may, ignited and infused with spirit and purpose.

Chapter One: Before the Revolution

AUGUST 25, 1967-APRIL 30, 1968

I.

253 days earlier:

The ocean crossing from New York had been rough but the early morning air was clear, with puffy white clouds set in crisp blue sky moving almost hypnotically out to sea. The SS United States eased its way into its berth at Le Havre. I still could not believe my good fortune. A whole year. In France. The clock starts now, August 25, 1967. The big black hull slid quietly along the quay then reached a full stop with a slight bump.

I thought of the initial rejection letter, received months before at Stanford. I had opened it late at night. The envelope had been skinny. Not a good sign. Sure enough, just a single sentence. I was disappointed but not surprised. My proposal had been a long shot.

Fast-forward to a week later, and imagine my interest at learning through the grapevine that the committee to award the grants had been so demanding that not all of the available grants had been awarded.

A thought formed. Why not? I looked up the professor who had chaired the committee in the University directory and arranged to meet with him. A conservatively dressed secretary ushered me into a wood paneled office, which was on the smallish side, in the oldest part of the Quad.

I said, "I have heard that not all of the grants were awarded."

He said, "That's true."

I said, "I wonder if my proposal could be considered again, now. I have heard that if scholarship grants aren't fully awarded, the available funds can shrink in future years."

He looked at me quizzically, smiled, then said: "Let me see what can be done."

I made sure he had my correct name and address and left optimistic. But I was stunned when I got the full acceptance package in the mail a few days later.

And the rest was history, as they say.

I did have some kind of obligation to the Fulbright-French Government scholarship program that was paying for me, but there was no rush about that.

I waited for the porter to gather my bags. An encounter with a real Frenchman again. I felt like taking a picture, but refrained. He wore blue coveralls and a work shirt. They were well-used but pressed and serviceable. He stooped for the luggage, an acrid burning cigarette hanging from his lower lip (*Gaulloise* from the smell, I guessed).

With the porter taking his sweet time I was emboldened and even dared to practice my French. "Quel temps fait-il?" (What is the weather) I asked as he scooted the bags onto the dolly.

He understood what I meant and was ready. He smiled, deadpan. "Il fait l'orage, monsieur". I smiled, not understanding the response, but making a mental note that it sounded like orange.

I followed the porter with my bags out of the stateroom and down the gangway to the pier.

All that coursework in French, and I still could not hold up my end of a casual conversation. I'd have to do something about that. I was vexed briefly. But excited even more at arriving.

The day was sunny but not too warm yet. Beautiful early autumn day. Too cool to be called Indian summer.

I was second in line for customs. I tipped the porter. He accepted the money, then turned brusquely away, without even so much as a thanks. I approached the kiosk. The officer in the booth motioned for my passport, I handed it over with some paperwork, which he studied in a half-interested way, chatting with a colleague in an identical booth nearby about things I did not catch, then stamped the papers and the passport and gave them back to me.

I had arrived at last.

II.

I made my way from French customs to the train station. The next train for Paris would be leaving on the hour.

I had spent five days and four nights in Paris during the previous summer, and could not wait to get back. I had fallen under the spell of the city on the very first evening. I had strolled from my cheap hotel in the Latin Quarter to the Seine and stood in front of a massive stone building, the dark, weathered and stained facade illuminated artificially, the ramparts from which I imagined Roman generals addressing crowds. The building turned out to be

Notre Dame, but by the time I found out, I was too far gone to have cared much. I had fallen in love. With a stone facade. And a city.

I vowed to return some day and live there.

And so it had come to pass, the very next year, at the height of the Vietnam war, and me of prime draft age.

After a lengthy train ride from Le Havre to Paris, I took a subway to the suburbs, where I had been invited to stay temporarily with the family of B. R. I had worked under him in a tiny two-person Brussels law firm during the previous summer where he had been the sole associate. There had been three of us working as unpaid summer interns, myself, Robbie, and Charles, each given room and board in the large house/office of H. A., who was the (other) head lawyer. We had been offered free tickets aboard an international air carrier who was a client of H.A. as an added inducement. Even though there was no salary or other compensation, the opportunity to work on significant international law problems in a small firm sounded like an ideal opportunity, so between the unique work experience and travel, I had grabbed at the chance. I saw quite a bit of Europe on the way over, making stops in England, Scotland and Holland before arriving in Brussels, and did some more sightseeing during a break I took in the middle of the summer to Paris.

Once in Brussels, you got to H.A.'s establishment by taking a street car along a wide and staid boulevard. It was bordered by park areas along the route. The sunlight seemed filtered through a layer of gauze. It rained a lot. His house was multi-storied, of red brick. The ground floor was his law office. H.A. lived upstairs and had his own office up there too. He had no family, as far as I can recall. B.R. lived with his family elsewhere. B.R.'s own office was on the main floor. The kitchen and living room were there too.

We interns occupied the basement. We bunked dormitory style and had our own bathroom. We were expected to report for duty in a large common workroom with a large table, also down in the basement. I suspect the workroom also doubled as a conference room if need be when there were no interns about.

About a month after we began, I found Robbie pacing in the workroom, his brow furrowed angrily.

"What's up?" asked I.

"This is not lawyer's work. This is something a bookkeeper should be doing, taking care of his household expenses. It's the straw that breaks the camel's back. I am sick of it, plain sick of it."

He showed them to me.

"I don't want to do them either," I said. "Charlie, come here, take a look at this."

Robbie was going into his last year at Boalt Hall Law School in Berkeley. Charlie was from Columbia; I was at Stanford Law. H.A. had gotten the cooperation of the schools by presenting himself as a benefactor and his program as a scholarship in international law.

"Let's go as a group to B.R.," said Charlie.

We trudged up the well-worn stairs and went down the wood floored hall to B.R.'s office. He had an open door policy.

"What's up?" he greeted us cheerfully. "Sit down, sit down." He was young, scarcely a year or two older than us, so it seemed, though he had to be considerably older, given how long he had already been out of school. He took out his pipe, which was already loaded up, and kept it unlit in his hand. (He was trying to cut down, he explained from time to time.)

Robbie spoke. He explained the problem, tight-lipped. "I don't mean to sound ungrateful but this job opportunity was sold as a unique opportunity to do actual international law work. It hasn't turned out to be that, just boring routine matters. Certainly, it should not also include keeping track of H.A.'s personal finances. It is demeaning and outrageous," he concluded.

B.R. put his forehead in one hand as a gesture of exasperation.

"I'm sorry. He ran it past me last week and I thought he was on board to keep the bookkeeper, in fairness to you boys."

Charlie spoke up, incredulous. "You mean, if he can get us to do this for free, he no longer needs to pay a bookkeeper to do it?"

B.R. wasn't prepared to go that far and he pulled back slightly, then sighed.

"Let me take this back to him. Let him know how we all feel. Remind him of what's important here. In the meantime, nobody has to do it. How's that?"

We looked at each other.

"Fine," said Robbie, still hot under the collar.

"Tell you what?" replied B.R. "How about you boys come over to our house tomorrow night for a home-cooked American meal? Take a night off, huh?"

Robbie let out a deep breath, willing himself to relax. "Yeah, sure, B.R. Thanks. Thanks."

It turned out, as B.R. later reported, H.A. had just unilaterally changed his mind and was stubbornly sticking to it. If anyone objected, they could pay for their own ticket home. Not the first time that threat had been brandished.

The evening was good though. The food and company were great.

Despite H.A., or perhaps because of him, we felt like a band of brothers.

B.R. and his wife, a pretty young woman from California, were sincerely looking forward to my Paris visit, and I was too, but it did not go particularly well. They were very warm to begin with, but without the common misery of H.A.'s dictatorial rule, it soon became apparent that we were embracing very different worlds. I was embarking on an adventure as a Parisian student, which to me was exotic and daring. I was impatient to begin. They had recently relocated to Paris and were pursuing a middle class life of aspiring lawyer and housewife/mother in a foreign land where she spoke passable but not fluent French. It seemed to be very difficult for her. They were isolated. She was home-bound with the kids and chores. He worked hard and had to commute. They were exhausted.

I slept in a guest bedroom of their apartment, which was relatively spacious for Paris and nicely furnished. The kids attended an

American school, but child rearing was difficult for B.R.'s wife without domestic help, which they did not want or could not afford. My very presence disrupted their routine. It became clear after a few days that the arrangement was not working.

I took a cheap hotel room in the Latin Quarter and registered with the Prefecture of Police as a student, the University's Paris Law Faculty II as a doctoral candidate, and a local student organization as a foreigner, all according to the instructions in my scholarship packet. One good natured French girl at the reception desk of the student organization helped me to find a low-rent apartment at the edge of the student quarter, in the working class neighborhood of Les Gobelins. It was located at one end of an ancient marketplace, which dated from medieval times. The market was open for business most every day, and was located along the Rue Mouff'tard. I walked it each time I went to classes and back.

It was mostly narrow, with small shops and stalls. There were butchers, bakers, hardware shops, restaurants, cloth shops, cooking utensils suppliers, spice and nut merchants; you name it, you could probably find it there or by asking someone in the market how to get it.

People stood entrances of many of the shops and stalls calling in a cacophony of sing-song refrains "Allons-y Messieurs, Dames. Allons-y. Il y a que du bien, il y a que du bien." (Come on, Ladies and Gents, there is nothing but the best, nothing but the best.)

I met the owner of the apartment by appointment. He had just renovated it. He had remodeled it mostly by himself on a very limited budget and the extra income was obviously important to his family, small as the place might be. He had a mustache, shirtsleeves, and rough pants, held up by suspenders. The studio was a single room, cramped, with fresh wallpaper and a cheap sink and miniature shower on the top floor of a five story walk-up. There would be just enough room for a single bed and tiny dresser. The lavatory was shared. It had a Turkish toilet, which is a hole in the floor with porcelain foot supports instead of a toilet and seat, a tank and chain to flush, and a water faucet but no sink. You brought your own paper with you. It was located off the hallway, and was shared with two girls, whom I never saw.

But who left little gifts. Like occasionally unflushed body waste and, a couple of times, used sanitary napkins.

Not the best neighbors. I yelled a protest through their door one time, when they did not answer my knock and I thought I heard someone inside, but nothing changed in that department.

There was a space heater powered by bottled gas.

The small flat had a window that looked out over a schoolyard. It was a recess break and school kids played in the yard below, across the way.

The apartment itself was clean and unpretentious. It had a view of ancient sooty Parisian chimneys emerging from plastered peaked roofs as far as the eye could see. We settled on the price and I moved in. But it was too small and uncomfortable to remain in for long, so I mainly used it for sleeping. I bought a small bed, a cheap dresser, a hotplate, saucepan, and a couple of dishes and utensils. I occasionally ate there but most often went to a student restaurant not far away from the Law Faculty, which was located about 10 minutes away on foot, at the Place du Panthéon, which was also on the left bank.

The first time I went to the student restaurant I waited in line with a throng of fellow students. It was dusk. No one spoke to me and I was shy. At the appointed time the doors opened and the students literally poured in, spilling up a flight of wide stairs and deposited like driftwood on the tide into a large room with common tables. I sat down at a table with six to eight other students. Several chatted with their friends. The others kept to themselves, quiet. I tried to make small talk, but my limited language skills and the impersonal atmosphere soon discouraged me. I ate my meal in silence.

A lunch or dinner in the student restaurant cost less than 80 cents US and consisted of several courses that usually tasted pretty good, but the experience was lonely.

I bought a French-only *Robert* dictionary and daily editions of *Le Monde*. At the beginning of the year, usually every morning, I would buy a newspaper, select one article from the issue, and circle words that I did not really understand. I looked these up in the dictionary. I tore out and saved each article having circled words. After a week or so, I went back to old ones, looked at the circled words, and tried to recall what they meant from memory alone. If I could not remember, I looked them up again. Usually it never took me more than two times to accurately remember a circled word. This process expanded my vocabulary quickly.

But spoken French was still not coming easily, so I posted a notice on a bulletin board outside the student restaurant in a café annex where students could hang out after a meal and visit over coffee. I got a response the next day. Someone had scrawled a note over my notice inviting me to meet in the café in the mid-afternoon when the crowds usually thinned out.

I found him at a table, alone. We exchange pleasantries. He was about my age, 25ish, and wore a dark green sweater and purple corduroy pants, neither of which looked new. His dark hair was cut short and was askance, uncombed. He was short and wiry. He had stubble on his chin. His front teeth were stained. He smoked *Gaulloise* cigarettes and drank espresso. He was lively, very chatty, quite intelligent, and liked to laugh. I caught a fair amount of what he said, but not all. He related that he was preparing to be a school teacher so tutoring me in French suited him. I asked if he spoke English and he replied with difficulty, moving his jaw in an uncomfortable way, as though working on a jawbreaker candy. He managed finally to spit out the phrase. "I do not speak English very well." He ended it with a laugh. When I told him I was American and not British, his brow knitted, and he asked me quietly and very seriously what I thought of the Vietnam war. I told him I was against it. His features immediately brightened, animated even, he thumped the table and laughed and exclaimed: "Excellent!" But when he realized I was not tracking everything he said, he returned to the essentials. He quoted a price of 10 francs (about $2.00) per lesson, which should in principle last about an hour, but who knew how long it would really last if it got interesting (his words), and we struck a deal. He gave me the address of his flat, which was nearby on the Rue Tournefort, drew a detailed map with directions on a napkin, and set a time for a first session. His name was Pierre Arènes, like the nearby Roman arena ruins, he added. "You know what these are, yes?" He suggested I bring my dictionary, to see if it was suitable for our collaboration.

I found the address at the appointed time. The street was narrow and cobbled, old, the once white facades of the two and three story buildings streaked with soot and grime, a quiet working class micro-neighborhood just off the Place de la Contrescarpe, which was a lively square in the student quarter filled with restaurants, neighborhood shops and cafés, with an overabundance of rude waiters and boisterous patrons.

I mounted the stairs of his apartment building to the second floor and knocked on a freshly varnished painted wood door. He opened it. He motioned for me to enter. It looked like he had just woken up, which was in fact the case, though it was 10 AM, our appointed time. He motioned me into the kitchen, where he was drinking café au lait from a bowl into which he dunked a section of a baguette cut in half and spread thinly with butter, took a bite, then sipped the contents of the bowl again. There was another used bowl and spoon still on the table, which he cleared. "Excuse me", he said. "Late night." He laughed, apologetic. "No, no", he insisted when I offered to come back another time, "no need".

"It is fine, really." Would I like some coffee? "No? Well, let me get some paper and a pen."

He disappeared into one of the bedrooms. The other door was shut. He came back.

Did he live alone? No, he had a roommate, a girl, Elisabeth. Were they a couple? No, no, just friends, roommates. Platonic. Nothing romantic. For about a year now.

He perused the dictionary and declared it to be suited to our task. "Look, look at this word. The etymology is correct. From the Latin.

Well done." He mused to himself, scratching his chin absentmindedly.

"It is better that you are using a French language dictionary than a French-English one. You will learn faster and better. More completely." He continue to nibble at the butter-smeared baguette, which he called a "tartine" and slurped his coffee from the bowl. When finished, he cleared the wooden table and wiped it off. The dishes were piled up in the sink.

"We switch off. It is Elisabeth's turn." He offered by way of explanation, though none was needed.

He motioned me to sit on the chair opposite at the table.

"So, here is how I propose we work: you will write a composition and drop it off. I will read it and take notes. Then we will meet to discuss it. You choose the subject. Anything you like. Maybe a page or two. Not more. But today of course we cannot do that. So let us talk and you can ask me questions."

"What is 'orange'?" I asked, recalling the exchange with the porter during the debarkation at Le Havre.

"Orange. It is a fruit. You cut it open, eat the pieces. Or squeeze it for juice." He chuckled and shrugged his shoulders opening his arms wide, as though to emphasize the simplicity of the question, wondering if there was more or if it was a riddle.

"No, wait, I mean, maybe 'orage'".

"Ah, l'orage." He opened the dictionary. "Here, you see. There are many meanings, but basically it is very bad weather. Lightning, thunder, wind, squall. You get the idea…"

"Not a nice day?"

"No, never. Do you understand?"

I did. Completely.

III.

The first composition was about my very first experience protesting the Vietnam War in San Francisco. I had gone there with a fellow law student A. K. and his wife. I was attending Stanford. I had never protested anything before, but I felt strongly that the War was obscene, an abomination. Silence was not an option.

I slid it under Pierre's door with a note that I would be available the next day to discuss it. I returned at the appointed time. He was at home. He had marked up the paper. It was about a page and a half long, handwritten. He seemed amused. He thought parts of it were hilarious for not only the malapropisms, but also the contents, and in other parts touching. We went through the grammatical errors and usage. He explained the use of the negative in French.

"You see, there are always two parts. First is the 'ne'. Then you have the qualifier. There is always a second qualifier. The two elements wrap around the verb that they negate. So, whenever you want to say not, you put the 'ne' in front of the verb and put the word 'pas' or other qualifier afterwards, like you are saying 'not' twice, but of course it is not so, you only say it once. Like 'je ne pense pas', meaning I don't think. The 'pas' originally was for emphasis. Like, 'not a pace'. You understand, like saying 'not even a tiny bit.' Then it became mandatory over time. You cannot say 'not' in its ordinary sense any other way today. Then there are other qualifiers. Each provides a different nuance; for example 'ne + guere' means scarcely. Or 'ne + goutte' which emphasizes an inability also, like I can't see a blessed thing, which is 'Je ne vois goutte'. The second word 'goutte' emphasizes the point. It actually comes from a mistake because it originally came from 'Je ne bois goutte' meaning 'I am not drinking, even a drop' but the 'b' changed to 'v' over the course of time (the people then were not highly educated) and then the whole construction became a way of expressing the same hyperbole. Or 'ne + point' like no, full stop. Always there are two words used to express the condition of 'not'. You see, yes?"

I had left the dictionary at home, but he was encyclopedic in his knowledge of the origin and derivation of French phrases.

His roommate Elisabeth came in near the end of the lesson. I was dumbstruck. She was beautiful in a classically Gallic way, with coiffed, shoulder length wavy blonde hair, blue-grey eyes, sculpted features, and a sophisticated, self-possessed manner. She wore a navy blue short sleeved sweater blouse and a blue and tan plaid knee length narrowly pleated skirt with a tan leather belt that showed off her figure. They chatted briefly about goings-on in their lives; she was vivacious and witty, and then Pierre introduced me. She nodded perfunctorily, as though as one of his students, I was hardly worth knowing, or perhaps she resented the intrusion of a lesson into her personal space, then went to her own bedroom and closed the door. Pierre noticed the effect she had on me and my total lack of effect on her but said only "ummm," under his breath.

We finished up and I paid him the ten francs for the lesson. He accepted it but told me with a mischievous grin that he had a confession to make. He could no longer take money from me. We had developed a friendship, he said. He didn't care. He would teach me for free after this. I protested but he was firm.

I was grateful for Pierre's friendship. The city was lonely and there was little other opportunity for social interaction. No one had been friendly, except Pierre.

There was one table in the student restaurant that was consistently lively though. The same group met meal after meal, some of them pulling chairs away from other tables and doubling around. And the prettiest girls in the place were among them.

They gathered, too, after meals in a café that adjoined the restaurant, which was an extension of it. They were a clique, and one day I was surprised to see Pierre laughing and chatting among them, one of the group.

He saw me and motioned me over. He introduced me as an American who was taking refuge in Paris from the Vietnam War. I was immediately welcomed like a brother by the table.

It was not entirely accurate to depict me as escaping military service, but I let that one go by. My draft board had actually granted me a second graduate degree deferment from the Vietnam War to pursue this scholarship opportunity in France, which was a stroke of luck. Otherwise I would have certainly been drafted into military service. Maybe I hoped that by letting the explanation stand, my plight would seem more dire than it was and my status around the table enhanced. Also any explanation was complicated and likely beyond my language capabilities.

Pierre went around the table making introductions. First there was Maurice, a bear-like fellow with glasses, shaggy hair and a long dark beard who smiled like the Buddha. He was presented as an intellectual authority on Marxism. He could cite volume and page by memory from the collected works of Marx and Engels on any theoretical proposition involving Communism, even footnotes.

Next came Jacques, of medium height, broad shouldered, a clean shaven type with a hint of stubble, shoulder-length blonde hair and a Jean Paul Belmondo good-guy anti-hero charm and charisma. He was a bit older, and definitely the leader.

Next to him sat Elisabeth, Pierre's roommate. She brightened in Jacques' presence, and behaved in subtle ways around him that seemed to suggest that they were intimate, or were about to be, I realized with dismay. She was a little friendlier to me than she had been at our first introduction, and had a sparkle.

Then came Pierrot le Fou (Crazy Pete), who talked way too fast and was generally manic. He spilled some of his coffee on the table as he emphasized a point, to the amusement of others. He shrugged and laughed it off good naturedly, then continued in his high strung way.

Across from him was Pierre T., a tall, mostly quiet fellow who could have been an accountant or bookkeeper. He was clean shaven and had short, neatly combed hair, a pressed white shirt, and properly creased slacks. He was quiet, thoughtful, perhaps shy.

Across from him was Suleiman, a well-dressed Algerian who introduced himself as a Maoist. He was handsome, slim, tall, with a dreamy air about him, and a polite, kind, empathetic manner.

There were others, too many to keep track of after the first few introductions, and more than a sprinkling of good looking girls.

The banter was jovial, the wise-cracks clever and funny, and the laughter genuine. They were a good group, tight, and they took care of each other in that special way that young people sometimes do.

I grabbed a chair, sat down among them, kept mostly quiet, answering questions briefly, trying to follow the conversations, more or less successfully, painfully aware of my difficulty in expressing myself properly in French.

I was grateful to be included.

IV.

The Faculty of Law, Paris II, was a massive ancient multi-storied stone building with impressive history located on the Place du Panthéon. I climbed the marble stairs and found the lecture hall. There were hundreds of students. The professor entered and took the podium. He droned on about St. Thomas Aquinas, his views on law and philosophy, the Catholic doctrines he espoused or contradicted, and the influences on various areas of modern French law. It was terribly boring. I had trouble staying awake. When the class was over, the students filed out. I had not exchanged a word with anyone.

After class I made my way to the nearby Place de la Contrescarpe.

Le groupe (my name for the group or clique) met often in a café on the Place de la Contrescarpe called Chez Sadoul. It was small with maybe eight tables and enough chairs for four to six patrons per table.

I found a group of my new friends at a table and joined them.

The owner, Sadoul, was slim, slightly round-shouldered, with the the beginning hint of a paunch, mostly bald on top with brown longish hair gathered in a short pony tail in back that was peppered with grey streaks on the sides and back, and large sideburns mostly gone white. He wore an oversized white shirt, vest, slacks, which I guessed to be the bottom half of a man's suit, and suspenders to hold them up,. He was about fifty plus years old. He worked the bar with his son Henri, who looked to be in his twenties, quiet and sympathetic. Sadoul's mother also helped out. She was about 80, a woman who could have been carved from a weather-beaten plank. She liked to touch and let a hand linger on the biceps of young male customers on some pretext or other.

Sadoul said to me: "And you, young man, what will you be having?" His head leaned forward, the chin brooking no opposition, but the manner polite if somewhat impatient.

"Coffee, espresso" I said mumbling, not wanting to draw attention to my language deficits.

"What?" he said. "Speak up." He turned to the others at the table and asked, "What is with your friend? Is he deaf? Mute?"

A few laughed. "No, he is American."

"Ah," he replied. "The Americans." He shook his head in mock wonder as though being American explained something. He went behind the counter. "Sugar?"

"Yes please," I replied somewhat too loudly.

"Ah there," quipped Sadoul. "Your friend learns quickly. He may prove to be intelligent yet."

I replied, trying to sound competent, that I would like my espresso to be strong (bien serré), but it came out wrong.

"Perhaps not so quickly," said Sadoul judgmentally but not unkindly. "We shall see. We shall see."

He wiped off the counter.

"Maman. If you please, five espressos for these fine young gentle men and ladies."

And at the student restaurant, later, I happily took a seat at the table of the groupe.

"How did you find the faculty? No too fascist for you?" asked one the groupe, handing the basket of bread to me.

"Disappointing. The teacher was boring, the lecture hall was enormous, and there was no interaction with the professor," I reported. "Where I attended school, Stanford, we had mostly small classes. Like the telecommunications by satellite program of my last year. Engineers, other specialists, all working together. We were tasked a hypothetical satellite program. Our reports were the sole basis of the grades."

Martine, a server, passed by handing out entrées and sides to the various tables.

Conversation often stopped when she passed. She was beautiful. A real knock-out. From the Carribean. Mulatto. It was a special moment when she passed by. She wore hip high leather boots below the baggy apron and uniform that failed to hide the voluptuous lines of her figure. I never saw so many lolling tongues. She scoffed at guys staring at her as she handed out the courses.

"Too bad she likes to get stoned," said Jacques, after she had moved on. "She has a fine mind in addition to all the rest."

"I heard that," she called out over her shoulder.

"And she has excellent hearing as well," Jacques called back with a grin. She turned and flashed a smile.

The entrée was brains. Each serving was a complete brain, of something. The folds and lines were clearly visible. I had never seen them before. I took one on my plate, suspiciously.

"You've never had this before?" asked crazy Pete. "You should try it. It's good."

"Uhh, I don't know," I said.

"Then give it to me," he said impatiently. "I love them."

"Give me a moment, please." I took a blob of mustard, hoping it might help.

I was starting to get self-conscious; everyone was looking at me in anticipation.

I cut off a piece and examined it. It resembled a laboratory cross-section. I slobbered it in the mustard, and put in my mouth. I chewed it experimentally. It was rubbery, dry. The texture was not to my liking. There was so much mustard on it that I could not tell its taste.

"Not bad," I said aloud at last, but I was already eyeing the side dish of potatoes and onions.

"American education sounds superior to a French one," opined crazy Pete. "We just learn… useless stuff."

"It probably was superior in Switzerland, too, I think," added Jacques thoughtfully. "At least it seemed so."

"What, you don't think your 'program' was intended to benefit the capitalists?" asked Maurice the Marxist theoretician quietly, without raising his voice or getting excited, as if he was asking for the salt and pepper. "Weren't those students going to seek jobs after finishing their education? Become part of the capitalist economy? So what does it matter if your school was better? The excess labor value of the participating students simply was enhanced. It was just a more efficient exploitation of young student white collar workers. Not superior, not really, not at all."

"But perhaps there is another point to what he says," countered Jacques in all seriousness. "Enhanced efficiency logically should be a useful precondition to revolution."

"I thought the labor theory of value applied to goods, not services," I piped up, emboldened by what seemed to be a good language day in French for me.

"It can be either," replied Maurice, somewhat surprised that I knew the labor theory of value at all. "So you know something about Marxism. Where did you learn it?"

"In college."

"I thought Marx was banned in the States," said Maurice.

"No, not really," I said, unwilling to back down yet. "Let me ask you a question. What about the Soviet Union. Is that Communism as you see it?"

"Ah, there you touch upon something fundamental," commented Jacques, emphasizing the point with his fork.

"No, definitely not", Maurice replied. "The Soviet Union is not Communist. It is repressive, an example of state capitalism, in many ways worse than private capitalism."

A few of the other students checked their watches. The meal was almost over, and I got the impression they had heard this particular subject discussed before. Soon it was just me and Maurice left at the table, finishing up.

"Tell me," I asked, "When all is said and done, do you really believe all that?"

"Of course," he replied seriously, "Don't you?"

I didn't, but to be diplomatic, I said: "I was taught it like some quaint, historical theory. Very serviceable as abstract political thought and philosophy. But impractical and outmoded."

"Perhaps it will come alive for you now," he replied smiling, as we got up to bus our dishes. "It is for us."

V.

Summer gave way to autumn, with clear brisk days and interminable rainy ones, and a new rhythm of life. I did not know anyone who spoke English, so I was fully immersed in French. I began to find myself conceiving thoughts directly in French. I sometimes woke up thinking I had had a bad language day only to find I had been dreaming. In the morning I would take breakfast in a café, buy a paper and circle words in an article to review later in the dictionary. I would take lunch and dinner in the student restaurant where I usually would meet up with Pierre and other members of the groupe, and we would finish the evening discussing things in some café or other until it was time to turn in. The hours in between were filled with sightseeing, wandering, and reading. I tried to attend classes, but the lectures were insufferable, and I decided that I did not really want or even need another law degree. Eventually I started doing some work on my own for my scholarship program, meeting with officials, getting to know their agencies, understanding what was going on in European space programs and telecommunications by satellite, which was the subject I was supposed to be studying. The effort lacked the hard discipline of a high powered law school like Stanford that I was used to. It was more just satisfying my curiosity, or maybe laying the foundations for a possible job opportunity after the year in France was done.

Through other student friends, I met Michel, a red-haired taciturn youth from Brittany, who was proudly Breton. He was a devotee of the Paris Cinémathèque, an institution that showed both classic and cutting edge films for a very nominal fee. He invited me to accompany him. It was located in those days in the Palais de Chaillot across the river from the Eiffel Tower, not far from the Seine. For a brief while, I was frequent visitor to the Cinémathèque.

I remember seeing Bernardo Bertolucci's film "Before the Revolution" there, about a young man who becomes entangled with Marxist ideology and at the same time, begins an incestuous affair with an aunt, who is about 10 years his senior. He becomes distressed over a friend's suicide and disillusioned when the aunt-lover has sex with another man. In the end the protagonist goes back to his beautiful but empty-headed ex-girlfriend, who is probably going to marry him and turn him into a conventional bourgeois. The end.

We went in inclement weather and remarked on the precarious footing on the way back to the Trocadero Métro station, which seemed much farther from the Cinémathèque than it really was.

"We could almost ice-skate," said Michel. "If we had skates."

We finally reached the subway. It was a long ride back to the student quarter, but I really liked the Métro. It was clean, much cleaner than the London tube or the New York subway. I appreciated the wooden four seat benches, arranged like an old time carriage, and the way the doors opened and shut. It had a quaint charm.

We discussed the film.

"The main character is passionate for the revolution but is a bourgeois himself," ruminated Michel.

"Maybe he is a revolutionary who just happens to come from the bourgeoisie," I replied, playing devil's advocate.

"No," he replied, noodling the problem. "The fact that he leaves the relationship with his aunt to marry respectably shows he never was anything but a bourgeois. No courage of feelings or convictions. Not to be trusted to bring about the Revolution. Or perhaps he just lacks sufficient maturity. Then again the aunt is older and therefore more mature, but she lacks judgment, having cheated on him, so maybe maturity does not count for much either."

"Do you really believe a Marxist revolution is inevitable?" I asked.

"Perhaps not inevitable, but scientifically predicted." Michel replied. "We are all living Before the Revolution."

"But will a revolution necessarily take place? Maybe that is why he becomes disillusioned. He gives up waiting for something in vain."

"Do you believe it is an illusion?" asked Michel.

"Before I came here I thought it was a quaint if outmoded idea."

"And now?"

"I am not so sure."

"Then perhaps you shall find out for yourself," concluded Michel amiably.

The Métro wheels went clackety-clack, clackety-clack.

VI

The first big manifestation (political demonstration) took place a few weeks later. It was organized by leftist French students denouncing the Vietnam War, a solidarity march with American protesters. It wasn't as though France had sent troops, but the US had inherited the mess from the French, so there was history there. And France still had a black eye among leftists for its brutal anti-insurgency repression in Algeria, which had ended a decade earlier, and brutality against the local population was one of the most hated aspects of American intervention in Vietnam.

The demonstration was set to start along the Quai d'Orsay, near the National Assembly and Bourbon Palace, traverse the Seine River at the Pont de la Concord, and continue from there to the US embassy.

I was sitting at a table with the groupe. Elisabeth said: "You should go. Just to see it." She twirled a lock of blonde hair between the thumb and forefinger of one hand, absent-mindedly.

That was the first time she had directed a comment to me. I looked at her.

"Or not," she added quickly. "As you like. It is all the same to me."

I asked if anyone would like to join me, but I got no takers.

The police had blocked the route and the demonstration was stalled for more than a half mile along the Quai. The wind off the river was cold. People were stamping their feet and blowing their hands just to keep warm.

I made my way to the head, along the edge of the crowd of marchers, picking my way along, muttering in French like a litany, "Excuse me", "Sorry", "Thank you".

At the front, a spectacle played out. Police in riot gear blocked the way from the Palais Bourbon to the bridge. They wore black helmets and uniforms and carried oversized shields, to protect the body and head, with wire cages extending down from the helmets in front of the face, a little like a catcher's mask in baseball. Gas masks hung loosely from their vests. They had large black batons. Large black vans, dozens of them, were parked behind the police, lined up, in a kind of security perimeter.

Tough looking protesters with batons of their own and motorcycle helmets both kept order among the demonstrators and faced off against the police. The street lamps lent a stark light that cast deep shadows.

This was definitely organized. Much leaner, meaner and more determined than anything I had seen in the States.

At the front of the police command post was a head man in authority in a full length overcoat and dark felt hat. He was talking animatedly with a rough and scruffy delegation of protesters. They seemed to be negotiating. The mood of the demonstrators was getting uglier by the moment. It was freezing cold and the wind blew off the nearby river incessantly.

Finally, an agreement was reached, and the crowd of protesters surged forward like water spilling from a breached dam. The police retreated, presumably deploying and taking up stations further along the route.

The demonstration moved steadily on. I dodged into a Métro station long before it reached the Embassy. I was too cold and had seen enough.

VII

The first party I was invited to as a member of the groupe was coincidentally held in April, several nights after news broke that Dr. Martin Luther King had been assassinated. The US was engulfed in riots and protests.

It put a damper on it for me.

Somebody's parents were rich and out of town. The bash was held in a large apartment in a fancy neighborhood. There were ample balconies with stupendous views of the river and the city. Booze and wine flowed.

I went out onto a balcony. The weather was clear and cold, typical for early April, so I had been told. I smoked a cigarette alone, in thought.

"It makes you sad?"

I turned and saw Elisabeth, ambling slowly, almost glidingly, towards me. The moonlight cast alabaster highlights and gray shadows across blonde hair, features, eyelids, lips, figure.

"What?"

"The death of the black leader, King?"

I shrugged. "Some."

She paused and leaned against the railing, next to me, facing me.

"What, you see it as some revolutionary necessity?" I asked.

"Boof," she waved a hand dismissively with a wry smile, glancing downward.

She motioned for my cigarette, I handed it over and she inhaled deeply, then handed it back, and looked out in the same direction as me.

And yet I had seen and heard her passionately immersed in political discussion and theory.

"There is a time and a place for everything," she said, turning towards me, as though replying to my thought.

She leaned fetchingly against the railing again.

"You find it interesting here?" she asked, then continued without waiting for an answer, "I think the US is more interesting. Bigger scale, center of everything, even Vietnam, racism. More and bigger evils to oppose. The place where a revolution could have the most impact world-wide."

"We are ruled by old men like De Gaulle. They are the remnants of the resistance to the Nazis," she continued. "They hold us back. They are ..." she searched for the right word, 'artheriosclerotic.'"

"As a result, France is sadly reactionary," she concluded.

She paused, then looked over at me.

"Sometimes I even imagine my own father as one of them." she finished.

"You have an easy relationship with him, then?" I asked.

One eyebrow cocked ever so slightly, she leaned forward, and asked, with a wry smile and a scoff, "You think?"

She turned gracefully and walked away slowly, looked over her shoulder languidly at me one last time, as though being held back by my gaze. She went inside, and, through the window, I saw her sit back down next to Jacques, and relax her body and surrounding space ever so subtly in his direction. He continued his train of thought unabated. Unconsciously, he shifted his body slightly towards her.

I was left outside under the night sky with lust as my only company.

Pierre saw the exchange. He came up to me and asked simply: "Unrequited love or vanity?"

"How can one be sure?" I asked.

"Well said," he replied.

"Ready to split?" I asked.

"Sure."

We said good-byes and left.

On the way to the Métro, a homeless man came up and asked for money. I had never seen homeless people before coming to Paris. (This was prior to Ronald Reagan, but that is another story).

Pierre said to him, "What do you need?"

The man replied, "It's freezing."

I silently agreed with that.

Pierre took off his coat and wrapped it around the man's shoulders.

"But what will you do?" he protested.

"Don't worry about it. I am fine. See, it is not even that cold. It is springtime." And to me, with a grin, "in Paris."

The man was touched. "Thanks, pal."

"Nothing," said Pierre, walking nonchalantly away. I caught up with him. He looked over his shoulder every few paces, until the man was out of sight.

"Hurry," he urged, jogging. "I am freezing to death."

I caught up with him again.

"You're nuts," I told him. "What are you going to do now for a coat?"

"I'll find something, trust me," he said assuringly. "Don't worry. He needs it more than I do."

Chapter Two: Police Brutality and Closure of the Faculties

MAY 1- MAY 12, 1968

I

It was already the beginning of May and spring was still coming teasingly. We sat in the outside terrace of the café La Chope on the Place de la Contrescarpe. The afternoon sun warmed us but the air was still chilly.

"What?" said Pierre suddenly, his head whipping around. "What was that you just said?"

He was addressing someone at the next table. I could not hear the conversation clearly and was having a bad language day anyway. The words stuck in my mouth and I could not process everything that was being said in French.

Pierre turned back to the table. "There it is. It has begun. The crazies at Nanterre have been thrown out of the Faculty. Some are being expelled or arrested. The bureaucrats have closed the School to all students."

"What are they protesting about?" I asked, bewildered.

He regarded me patiently, like a slow relative, and then answered, in a tempo that began slowly and steadily quickened, "Over-crowding of facilities, a mind-numbing curriculum. Inadequate training for job skills. A life as a consumer of stupid articles after graduation if one is lucky. A meaningless future however it turns out. The basic issues facing all of us. Got it?"

I just shook my head in frustration.

"Good," he said. "Let us go now and see what is happening."

That sounded better to me.

We wound up walking to the Champs du Mars near the Eiffel Tower, following groups of other students, milling about in a crowd once we got there, some people in the center talking passionately through megaphones and portable loudspeakers, Hyde Park style.

On the way over, Pierre's attitude softened and he explained more to me.

"Nanterre is another faculty, a newer one. They have a group there of leftists who are a little crazy."

"How so?"

"They had a riots there last year protesting separate girl dormitories. Wanted to have men and women share the same facilities."

"Like you and Elisabeth?"

"Exactly, it may be legitimate, I'm not saying it is not, but there are more pressing social issues to address."

"Maybe someone just wanted to get laid."

"Could be," he replied, with a sideways grin. "More power to them, then."

Pierre caught the attention of a couple of passers-by and stopped to catch up on the latest developments.

"The dean of Nanterre has closed the Faculty in response to continued student demands," one of them reported. "It is a potpourri of things but it is seriously Marxist and foreshadows a revolt, I'll bet."

"Students are marching on the Sorbonne in a sympathy move with Nanterre, students are marching on the Sorbonne in a sympathy move with Nanterre" shouted someone suddenly through a megaphone, repeatedly.

The crowd set off in the direction of the Sorbonne. Police sirens honked and moaned their particular French sing-sing refrain distantly but otherwise all became quiet. The crowd walked faster, as though responding to increased tension in the air.

Pierre explained more rapidly, but in a lowered tone of voice: "The Nanterre leftists are situationists, similar in many ways to us. They reject both Stalin and Lenin's theories about the need for a dictatorship of the proletariat."

"Trotskyites?" I asked. I had done a paper in school on the judicial system in the period post October revolution of 1917 and had a vague idea about Trotsky's later troubles with Stalin in the 1920's, ending in his assassination in Mexico by Stalinist agents.

"No, and you should never utter that term lightly," said Pierre in a subdued tone. "Trotskyites are hated almost universally in France by other leftists. There are even closet Trotskyites who are afraid to admit what they are. Bantering that word around imprudently in the wrong places could cause you grief."

"Anyhow, Trotskyites believe in the dictatorship of the proletariat. They just think Stalin got it wrong because he is a crazy tyrant. We don't believe in a dictatorship by anyone over anyone else, ever."

"Anarchists?" I took another stab.

Pierre was becoming irritated by my questions, regarded me sideways, and said with a tone of finality, "No. We believe in a worker revolution, they do not. A true worker revolution arises organically out a precise situation. It will be democratic, starting in worker councils, without anybody dictating anything to anyone else."

"Look at that," he pointed. We were approaching the Sorbonne, where cordons of police were charging into arriving demonstrators with batons, beating and arresting people willy-nilly. Students, and others from other walks of life (including one old lady still clad in pajamas) were constructing a make-shift barricade. Other protesters energetically began removing the paving stones of the cobbled streets with iron bars. The cobbles were each massive, weighing several pounds each, and looked like they could land a lethal blow. The same type of police vans and policemen from the Vietnam protest were being deployed near the barricades. A confrontation soon took place, with paving stones being launched over the barricade onto the police who protected themselves against the stones with large shields and helmets with wire cages to protect the face. When a first volley of paving stones ceased, the police responded by throwing tear gas grenades at the demonstrators, many of whom sprouted bandannas as improvised gas masks.

Pierre and I retreated in a crowd of participants and onlookers, most of us choking.

"Come this way, quickly," said Pierre. He ducked into a little side street a few blocks long. It was quiet except for the distant sirens, shouts of the demonstrators and exploding grenades. For a brief moment the sweet smell of a bakery's pastries could even be detected.

II.

The next morning, bright and early, the Government announced a "get tough" policy against the students.

The groupe took coffee with breakfast bread together at Chez Sadoul, exchanging information from the night before.

"The police are still arresting large numbers of students."

"High school students are on strike and are marching in the suburbs in sympathy with us."

We heard the sounds of unified chants, far away.

"Here it is. Let's go."

We paid up hurriedly and joined others in the street making their way towards the sound, drawn as if by a magnet.

Closer, the chant was "Long live the Paris commune."

The people possessed a quiet dignity, drawing taller in themselves as they funneled through the streets towards a vaguely understood destiny.

Then the spell broke and there were police and crowds and sounds and fury all around. We fell in behind other marchers who were singing the Internationale, but almost immediately the crowd broke up ahead and black uniformed shielded and baton wielding police came charging at us.

"Hold your ground!" came a shout from behind, where resolute arm-in-arm students several ranks deep stood ready to take the brunt of an attack.

We were caught in between, and scattered to the sides as best we could, falling back to regroup behind the front line. The police halted and were reinforced. The two lines faced off against each other.

A loudspeaker blared: "Disband, by order of the President of the Republic. Disband at once. All who do not are breaking the law and will be treated accordingly. Disband."

"Screw you!" came a shout, and derisive laughter.

Police charged again but the crowd melted in their path and they discovered, too late, that they were in the range of pavers that began raining down on them from their flanks. One cobblestone hit a policeman on the helmet who collapsed. A second shower of pavers began. The police retreated, supporting their fallen comrade, who miraculously could still ambulate with assistance.

The police donned gas masks and began lobbing tear gas grenades. I had brought a scarf and secured it to protect my mouth and nose. We stood our ground, but finally I could stand it no longer and retreated to get air. I was choking and coughing, for a moment unable to orient myself as to the surrounding streets, but it passed quickly. Surrounded by strangers, I turned around once again. Some held hands as we marched forward, resolute, wills locked more firmly than limbs, marching for our side, come what may, ignited and infused with spirit and purpose.

III

I got back to the Place de la Contrescarpe in the late afternoon. It had not been the scene of a struggle yet. Barricades were springing up all over the place. There were five narrow streets into the Square, and each was guarded now by at least one or more barricades. Piles of paving stones were in readiness.

There was adrenaline in the air.

The owner and several uniformed waiters were out in front of one of the usually busier cafés, though there was little business now, trying to shoo the students away. One activist said darkly: "You'd better not be police informants, if you ever want to show your faces in this quarter again." The owner threw up his hands in disgust, muttering obscenities and retreated to the café. The waiters began to shutter the glass windows.

A pitched battle started after nightfall. Flashes of light as first tracers and then gas grenades exploded, a car on fire silhouetted cocked arms astride raised barricades throwing pavers on police below. Retreating, advancing, retreating again. Sirens. Shouts. A refrain of a chant from the crowd, defiantly begun, abruptly ends. More shouts. Clouds of smoke and chemical vapors, near invisible whitish fog in the night clinging to the pavement and then drifting higher in the breeze.

Confusion. Elation. The barricades held.

Three AM. The battle seemingly over, we met in a café off the Place, closed to the public but opened to us. Self-congratulatory. Our side had prevailed. The police had not taken the Place de la Contrescarpe or expelled the demonstrators.

Pierre motioned to me. "There's Dani the Red," (so-called because he was a redhead as well as a self-proclaimed Communist). It was him, the student leader. Daniel Cohn-Bendit, a German student and a Jew, from the 22nd of March movement that had spear-headed the revolt at Nanterre. Spokesman for the ideology of a modern existentialist social revolution that was now coming to life in the quarter. The baddest-ass student of them all. Biggish of stature and frame. Dominating presence.

Cohn-Bendit and a couple of what looked to be his lieutenants sat down at the table facing off with Jacques, who was flanked by others who were mostly strangers to me. It seemed to me that Jacques was the spokesperson or leader of the group on his side of the table. At first each leader jockeyed for position verbally, then got down to business. I was not close enough to hear and understand all of what they were saying but they seemed to be on the same wavelength. Elisabeth sat next to Jacques, a little behind him, listening intently, saying little, drinking it in, totally present, laughing from time to time appropriately and appreciatively, more a silent partner. Cohn-Bendit, eyeing her from time to time. Me, seeing him watch her.

The morning papers were being delivered as the meeting broke up. "500 arrested", blared one headline.

"Student revolt!" said another.

We emerged from the café as dawn was breaking. Rose-purple and orange tones illuminated high clouds along their undersides. A bird sang. The air was warmer. It promised to be a beautiful spring day.

Jacques lit a cigarette.

An early riser was walking a poodle on a leash among the litter of the barricades and upended pavers.

Street cleaners were standing about, discussing how to tackle the mess.

We heard the sound of sirens in the distance. Jacques chuckled, knees bent slightly, a wry smile on his face.

"What, again?" he exclaimed. "I'm exhausted. What say we give it a rest?"

"No argument there, boss."

He punched the speaker playfully in the arm. "No bosses, no masters, remember?"

"Yes, boss," came the reply.

"Bof, sounds like an ambulance anyway," said another, with a thick Parisian accent and blasé manner that passed for cool.

A few milled about but I was bushed. I cursorily waved a goodbye to all, and headed straight to bed.

IV

Everybody must have worn themselves out, including the cops, because there was an uneasy peace in the Quarter for a couple of days.

I had been invited to dinner at the home of a couple in their late forties or mid-fifties. I had met the wife during one of my days pursuing the grant project. She worked as a director in the French patent office. I had contacted her for an interview, during which we had started talking about the Soviet Union and Franco-Soviet cooperation on technology matters. She had been critical of US restrictions on technology exchange with the East, I guess that she had found me to be a curiosity, so she had invited me to dinner at home with her and the hubby.

When she found out I was interested in knowing something about French cooking, she offered to demonstrate how she was going to prepare our meal. She invited me to show up a little early for that purpose.

They lived off the Boulevard St. Michel in a gracious apartment with an encompassing view of the Boulevard and a square. It had been in the family a long time, from before the Second World War.

I arrived with a bottle of wine which the husband graciously accepted but opened one of his own and poured me a glass. He was all ears and wanted to know where I came from, what I was doing in France, the usual. He was a professor. They had no children.

She called out from the kitchen for me to join her. He graciously waved me in that direction.

The kitchen was of sufficient size for serious cooking and she was busy preparing a salad, meats, some side dishes and various cheeses.

"We are going to have a rather simple meal," she began apologetically. "I work and don't have much time. But the classic order of a French meal is a good place to start, so let us begin."

She talked as she worked.

"Hors D'oeuvres come first. They stimulate the appetite. We are not having any tonight. Sorry."

"It's okay, My appetite is already stimulated," I assured her.

"Good. Next, L'entrée. You know it means entranceway. The meaning in relation to the order of food should be self-evident. We will have escargot. You know them?"

"I know of them. I have never eaten them." I said.

"Ah, then you are in luck. You know, the process of preparing them from scratch is quite laborious. They are toxic. Measures have to be taken to get rid of the poisons in their digestive systems. Some people feed them flour for several days. Others, salt. When they are ready, they are boiled, and the flesh is removed from the shell. It is mixed with a sauce. Traditionally in the north of France, it is made of butter, garlic and herbs, but there are many types of sauces by region. For instance in the south, it may be tomato-based. The mixture of sauce and snail is stuffed back into the shell."

"These we are having come already prepared from the store and you just heat them up in the oven. There is nothing to it."

"A fish course after the entrée is optional," she continued. "We will not be having this."

"A palate cleansing sorbet is sometimes served to cleanse the palate."

"Let me guess," I said. "Not tonight?"

"You are a very apt pupil."

"Then there is a main course, usually meat or poultry accompanied by a simple vegetable that is in season. It is this way because we buy the food fresh each day. It comes straight from the farm to the markets. It is much better than putting preservatives in the food to improve shelf life, but of course food shortages develop more quickly if the farmers go on strike, which happens from time to time. We will be having escalope de veau a la crème fraîche et l'estragon (Veal cutlet in a sauce of clotted cream and tarragon). It is quick and easy to prepare, minutes only. You should be able to do this at home yourself."

"Home is pretty small with only a hotplate," I observed.

"It should be enough to make the dish, if you can melt butter," she said. "And we will have a side of steamed green beans in a sauce."

"Next comes the salade, simple lettuce tossed with vinaigrette to cleanse the palate and aid digestion. We will use this," she said, lifting a head of lettuce to demonstrate.

"Finally, a selection of cheeses is served on a wooden board. You know cheeses?"

"I know Swiss, American and Cheddar," I said.

"Oh we have so many of them in France. It would be good if you could learn to recognize a good selection while you are here," she advised.

"I am a simple student on a limited budget. Not likely to happen." I replied.

"Try this Camembert. You see, you press on top to gauge if it is ripe. If it is too stiff, it is not ready. If it gives way too easily, or feels runny it is overripe and the taste will be off. It must be like this one." She had me push gently on the top of the cheese to see how it felt. It gave, but not easily, and sprang back a bit when I let up.

"Lastly is an optional sweet dessert, served with coffee. Fear not, we have some cakes for this."

"Good," I said. "I like sweets."

"Who doesn't?" she replied with a smile.

"One thing always to remember about French meals: You should allow plenty of time. Also," she added, cutting a baguette into sections and putting them into a basket, "you must have bread, plenty of it. And wine," she added as an afterthought.

The veal cutlet was thin but she pounded it to make it even thinner. She heated butter in a saucepan, lightly sautéed the veal, then added the crème fraîche and tarragon to complete a sauce. It was done in minutes.

"Please, help me take these things to the table."

I did as requested.

We sat down to the entrée of escargot. I emptied the contents of one of the shells onto my plate with a little fork. It was not easy. I tasted it experimentally. It tasted like herbs, butter and garlic, with a rubbery morsel that contributed more texture than taste. I mopped up the remains of the sauce with some bread.

"It is very tasty," I complimented her. She seemed pleased.

During dinner a mob began gathering in the square below. We watched from the table.

"It reminds me of the War, when the Germans came, rounding up people on the square, all this activity," she said with a shudder. "Luckily we were not Jewish."

A confrontation with the police erupted. Suddenly there were paving stones in the air, cars overturned, some aflame, barricades erected, tear gas clouds, people fighting and running. We had a bird's eye view.

"Seeing it from above is so different from actually being on the ground," I remarked over a forkful of veal, which was remarkably tasty.

"How so?" asked the husband.

"You can see what the police are up to, strategies being played out. See, they are trying to split the crowd in two. Down in it, you are just reacting, now becoming part of an advance or then of retreat or whatever. Doing your little part, like an ant."

"Are there no strategies from the student protesters?"

"Not much from what I see from up here," I confessed.

"What is it about exactly?" asked the professor, his wife also anxious to know, as though I was a living specimen instead of a Greenhorn and newcomer to the groupe, which was my chief connection.

"A lot about Marxism. The coming Revolution. A change in mankind's attitude."

"Well the head of the Communist Party just denounced the students as spoiled children of privileged parents."

"As did the Socialist Party," chimed in the wife.

I raised my hands in front of me, as if to say that I understood, the denunciations created a conundrum, to be sure.

Then I began on the salad. The lettuce was fresh as though just picked.

"It's a lot about being robbed of a meaningful future," I said between mouthfuls. "At worst, you are exploited or become a throwaway, at best, a pampered slave to a system that takes away freedom in exchange for silly trinkets. They want to get the message to the blue collar workers that it is their struggle as well, they say the students are their natural comrades in arms. I don't know how to express it any other way."

"Is that how protesters in America feel too?" asked the wife.

"It is much less about ideology. A big difference is that here many young people hope to bring about a permanent change in society through Marxist revolution, separate and apart from the traditional Communist Party. In the States I think there are similar feelings, but, for example, the hippies from California believe in spiritualism, the power of love, expanded consciousness through drugs like LSD, free stores, food, flower power, those kinds of things, which are revolutionary in a sense but without ideology.

"There may be elements that are shared between them, though."

"Well," said the husband, nodding his head in agreement, "there is something to be said in all of that."

"Yes," continued the wife diplomatically, "but is it otherwise not an illusion, a youthful indulgence?"

"How does one ever know if anything is within reach or just an illusion?" I asked by way of reply. "Unless you try? Doesn't the result alone provide the answer?"

"My point exactly," continued the wife. "It is in succeeding that the real problems begin. And what then? Who decides? How does one govern?"

"I think that is the point," interjected the husband. "There will be no government, no need for one. Withering away of the State."

"Which is an unfailing recipe for a strongman to take over," said the wife, with a tone of conviction.

"And if it fails," she continued, "what will that prove? That we are all abject slaves? I don't believe it. We have at least some responsibility for our own happiness. We don't live under the Nazis any longer. No one has that kind of control over us today. France is still a democracy."

"Have any workers actually joined the students?" asked the husband, changing the subject as the cheese was being taken away.

"Not that I have seen for myself, though I have heard through the grapevine that workers have been fighting alongside students on the barricades. But who knows if that is just wishful thinking, and if it is true, how many really."

"I am surprised," I said to my hostess. "I thought you were much more left-wing leaning when we talked at the Patent Office about the Franco-Soviet cooperation."

"I do vote Socialist," she said. "But that does not mean I should accept things unthinkingly because they include leftist ideals or ideology."

"And I am equally surprised by you," she continued. "If you are not a believer in Marxist revolution, why do you participate in these demonstrations, which go beyond the specific goals of ending the Vietnam War and the rest?"

I had not really considered this point before.

"I guess that I am willing to give it the benefit of the doubt, for now. And I admire the courage and pluck of the students," I replied.

Espresso and small cakes suddenly appeared.

My hostess poured the espresso.

"Woops!" shouted her husband, commenting the action below. "Molotov cocktails. More of them. It is getting serious."

"You should spend the night here for safety," she offered. "We have a spare bed."

"I'll be fine," I reassured them. "But I probably should get going. It looks like it may be over soon, finally breaking up out there."

I sipped the espresso quickly, said goodnight, and made my way down to the street.

Outside the Square was already nearly empty and full of litter. Cars were overturned. Several were burning. Paving stones were clumped and left willy-nilly on curbs and sidewalks. Garbage cans were overturned in the gutters, as though the contents had been dumped into the street before being thrown at the police.

A tall, heavy-set elderly gendarme approached me, nightstick menacingly extended in front of him. He addressed me gruffly in Italian.

"I am not Italian," I protested in French, somewhat indignantly. He looked at me puzzled for a moment, then moved on.

I made a beeline in the opposite direction for the Métro entrance. Still mindful of my bad language days, I wondered briefly had my accent in fact sounded decidedly English, throwing him off? And why was he speaking Italian to me anyway? Did I look Italian?

I was grateful when I reached the Métro without further ado.

V

I crossed paths the next day with Jacques and Elisabeth at a street corner. It was late in the afternoon.

"Aren't you coming to the demonstration?" asked Jacques, his beige tinted glasses reflecting the rays of the sinking light. "It is in the other direction, this way."

"I am going with friends to la République by Métro, to join up with the larger demonstration when it gets there. They are going to make contact with workers, if we find any."

"Be careful," he warned. "Right wing thugs are infiltrating the demonstrators and throwing Molotov cocktails."

"That wasn't students?" I asked.

"No. Agitators."

We parted company and I waited for my friends at the entrance to the Métro station. No one else showed. I decided to go to République by myself and see if I could spot them.

When I got out of the Métro at la République, it was obvious that I was on a fool's errand. A mob had assembled all up and down the Boulevard. No one could have found anyone in that mess.

I began to drift in a direction away from the Métro and down the Boulevard, checking the situation out.

There were police vans parked in the cross streets, and cordons of riot police lined up in wait behind them.

The people in the crowd included poorer, working class folk. Some older women in dark dowdy dresses, men in rough worker clothing. Chanting, waving placards, milling about, moving in a general direction along the Boulevard. Suddenly there was movement from the police. They charged into the crowd, throwing tear gas and waving batons. With the rest, I ran, up a street, then across another. I was lost. I did not know my way around this part of town. I fell in with a small group of people. We ran until we were in a dead end. If the police came, we were sitting ducks.

A woman appeared in a doorway, and motioned for us to come inside quickly. I followed the others into a small passageway that led to a courtyard. We stood quietly, some crouching, hearing the sounds of heavy footsteps, shouts, gas grenades going off outside. We waited, quiet as mice.

When all sounds of activity ceased, the woman, probably a concierge of the building, peered out of the doorway to the street. Seeing no one, she motioned the all-clear signal to us, and we left. I mumbled a thanks to her as we exited.

The streets had cleared of people, though there was a lot of noise coming down the Boulevard, away from the Square, in the opposite direction.

I made my way to the Métro and back to the Latin Quarter, where the student demonstration was still massing.

I found Pierre and some of the others down by the river, at the edge of things.

"It was awful," I reported. "Sitting there waiting to be arrested or beaten, afraid, only saved by a Good Samaritan. No sense of unity, of purpose. Just isolated individuals, by chance in the same place at the same time. It was like we weren't even connected as humans."

"Now you are finally catching on. The power of collective action. We will make a revolutionary of you yet!"

"Come on, they are beginning to move."

We moved forward, chanting, but suddenly the people in front of us began moving backward, crushing us between them and the people behind.

"The cops are attacking!" came a shout from up ahead.

We beat a coordinated retreat as a group, as barricades began to spring up around us.

I smelled a whiff of the now familiar scent of tear gas and affixed my scarf in place.

We were in for it. For sure.

VI

By daybreak there was still no end in sight. The police attacked in waves, sporadically, then there were lulls for negotiations. Still the barricades held.

As the day progressed, so did the battles, but now the residents of the Quarter got involved. News coverage blared into the streets from radios held high at opened windows in the upper floors. We followed the moves of the police in real time. Residents tossed water from windows onto the clouds of tear gas, to disperse them more quickly. Food was distributed by strangers from doorways. Each kindness rallied our spirits. And there were more and more rough looking guys joining us, possibly workers. Everyone was getting worked up to a fever pitch. A spirit of revolution grabbed the people collectively and refused to let go, shaking us like a dog with a bone in its teeth, relentlessly holding on now that it had a hold.

Night fell and still the fighting continued. Molotov cocktails became as prevalent as pavers. At the Rue Gay-Lussac, below the level of the Place de la Contrescarpe, the police launched a concerted attack against a barricade. Bystanders and students alike caught in their path were beaten as the cops made a gas-masked advance. Finally, the air thick with tear gas, more police came around another corner, behind the barricade. Students were trapped. Some took refuge in doorways and courtyards, but the police searched the buildings from basement to rooftop and soundly beat anyone they found, before hustling them away in police vans.

We had been further up the street, able to escape. We headed uphill, towards the Place de la Contrescarpe. The police followed, slowed by the house to house searches and arrests.

The situation was spiraling out of control, according to the news. The government seemed to be losing its hold.

A good thing this is not the States, I thought. At least nobody is firing guns. Nobody is dead. Yet. As far as I knew.

The Communist Party leader did an about-face and supported the activists against police brutality, so the radio reported.

"They're just doing that to get ahead of the movement. They're afraid of being left behind," said one protester as we heard the news. Others murmured their agreement.

By daybreak of the second day of fighting, the number and frequency of police assaults became overwhelming. The barricades fell. Students fled on foot. The radios, still blaring from windows, reported house to house searches and arrests. About 20 of us retreated to Pierre and Elisabeth's apartment nearby. We huddled peering out the windows. Policemen armed with rifles came warily up the street in the early morning light. We hid.

"What will we do if they find us?" whispered one of the group.

"Leave it to me," I said quietly. "I will go out there and meet them."

I pulled out my American passport. "This should do the trick." I smiled. "And how can I help you, officers?" I pantomimed in English in my best Texas accent.

That generated a laugh that cut the tension.

"Wait here and be quiet." I pulled up a chair into the entranceway of the apartment and shut the bedroom doors. I left the light on.

Perhaps a half-hour passed, then I opened the door to the bedroom. One of the students watching out the window motioned for me to be quiet. Then he slowly relaxed.

"It looks like they have gone."

We waited another half hour quietly chatting in subdued tones.

"Pedestrians are coming into the street on errands. It looks like it is all clear."

We relaxed and left the apartment building by two's and three's. I was dog-tired and made straight for my place and to bed.

Chapter Three: Student Occupation of the Faculties

MAY 13-MAY 31, 1968

I

I woke the next morning, having slept through the rest of the day and night. I groggily got dressed and stumbled up to Chez Sadoul. I needed coffee badly. I bought a pastry in a shop along the way.

The café was nearly empty.

"None of the groupe here?" I asked Sadoul as I approached the counter.

He looked about, then frowned and shrugged his shoulders, as if to say "Do you see anyone?"

"Coffee," I muttered, not ready for him without it, not yet.

"There is talk going around about you," he confided as he poured the coffee into a cup and handed it to me. Seeing the pastry, he also provided me with a plate.

The coffee was burnt and stale.

"Remind me why I keep coming here?" I asked, groping across the counter for a handful of sugar cubes.

"A veritable John Wayne, in effect," he continued, ignoring the question.

"I didn't do anything, not really." I replied truthfully, sipping the evil brew for effect if not the taste. I took a bite of the pastry, to distract from the bitterness.

"Oh, of that I am quite certain," he agreed amiably. "They are calling you 'the American'", he continued in a confidential tone. "You are becoming famous."

"Enjoy," he concluded, turning away.

I was sure he couldn't have meant the coffee.

"Hey," Sadoul called to me suddenly. "There they are. Your friends."

Jacques, Elisabeth and Pierre were coming around the corner and saw me through window. They came in, animated.

"Have you not heard the news?" asked Elisabeth.

"Where have you been?" asked Pierre.

"Sleeping," I said to him, and to her "No I have not."

"The police have left the student quarter. They have abandoned the faculties to the students. It is crazy. It is like a fair."

"We just have come from the Sorbonne, it's wild," said Jacques.

"Oh come on, admit it," parried Pierre, teasingly. "It was beautiful, all those sayings and pictures." He drew his arms out in a dramatic flair: "Beneath the paving stones – the beach!"

"Ballbuster," replied Jacques amiably to Pierre.

"How about 'The most beautiful sculpture is a paving stone thrown at a cop's head?'" joined in Elisabeth as well.

"Like I said, completely nuts," concluded Jacques with a mock shrug, as though the point had been made for him by the other two.

"Come, we are going to the Faculty of Sciences to see what is happening. Join us," said Elisabeth enthusiastically.

I threw some change on Sadoul's metallic topped counter, glad for any excuse to abandon the coffee.

II

We strolled in the direction of the Faculty of Sciences at Jussieu. It was to one side of the Latin Quarter, near the Seine, one entrance facing the river. It was still chilly but the trees were starting to sprout new growth. The clouds moved quickly over the Seine, like a time lapse film sequence signifying sped-up passage of seasons.

I had never been to that particular Faculty before. It consisted of a cluster of very old buildings and sterile post World War II new ones, arranged mostly in a square, with facades of aluminum and glass, done in what seemed to be cheap construction. People were milling about, entering buildings, exiting, authoring, assembling and handing out leaflets, making speeches to each other, forming committees spontaneously, searching for building and room number so-and-so.

On the first floor was a circular staircase, with a small chain across its hand rails. Someone had affixed a cardboard sign to the chain with an arrow that said above it "Worker Student Commission." The chain hung by one end only. The sign was lopsided. But at least the cockeyed configuration made the arrow point up the stairs.

I told the others I was going to take a look.

The stairs led to a large lecture hall, almost an auditorium. There were seats on either side and a large central floor area where additional seats or demonstrative exhibits could be set up, but the floor was empty except for some litter. There was a speaker area down in front and two raised portions with wood paneling on either side suggestive of wings in a theater. To each side, in the wings, stood one guy, in street clothes. They faced and preached political doctrine and theory to each other across the empty room, in kind of an improvised dialogue. I had seen this pair in action before in the quarter. I did not know their names but referred to them simply as Fric and Frac.

FRIC: "The purpose of the universities is to train specialists through mass production methods of degenerate capitalism. Students have been rendered incapable of independent thought. Teachers propagate this system by repressing critical thinking. Administrators enforce the system by hiring complicit teachers and firing authentic ones. Factory bosses contribute to the political campaigns of the politicians who reinforce the administrators. Higher education is a rigged system.

"All power to the people!"

FRAC: "Curriculum is designed to output workers as machines. Daily life outside of work is designed to create consumers of the products of capitalism. The whole of society is a grand spectacle to consume, work, and be exploited by the few at the top who control all. It is mind numbing and soul killing.

"Long live a true student worker revolution!"

FRIC:"The working class will spontaneously seize power. Worker councils will direct the revolutionary actions. There will be no dictatorship of the proletariat of any kind: Stalinist, Troskyite, Maoist or other. Down with these degenerate theories. All power to the worker student alliance!"

FRAC: "Unions have betrayed the rank and file for their own safety and gain. The Communist and Socialist parties are part of the system, initiators of the corruption, with stained hands. Workers: unite against the bosses of trade unionism as well as capitalist enterprises."

FRIC: "So-called respected intellectuals and artists sell their works for ambition and fame, feeding the system's voracious appetites, seducing the populace, becoming part of the festering problem. Artists: reclaim your true creativity: Work for the revolution instead!"

The room was bereft of an audience, but this did not deter their enthusiasm. I had heard their routine before, and it all seemed recycled to me, so after listening for a moment or two, I descended the stairs.

I strolled through the remainder of the first floor, navigating the bustling ad hoc activity without any seeming organization, pitching in to help fold some leaflets that had been printed in another faculty nearby, then I headed back to the Place de la Contrescarpe. I caught up with Pierre and Elisabeth.

The three of us took coffee on the terrace at La Chope, a much larger establishment on the Place de la Contrescarpe not far from Chez Sadoul. Tables and chairs outside extended almost into the street.

Elisabeth was very quiet, lost in thought.

Pierre asked, sympathetically, "Why the long face?"

She looked at him and said, somberly, her eyes now more grey than blue, "Today at the Sorbonne, in the courtyard, I saw a girl, up front, center, holding a flag high. She was the very face of the Revolution itself, a real Marianne." She paused, reflecting, then said simply, matter of fact: "It was mind boggling."

"Mind boggling?" inquired Pierre.

"The thought that it is becoming, real," replied Elisabeth softly, carefully choosing her words, taking a sip of cappuccino and lighting a cigarette. "That we could, that I could do, the same."

"Like a prophesy?" teased Pierre, but she did not laugh.

Instead she took a puff, twirled a lock of hair between the fingers of one hand, and remained contemplative. Then she turned to Pierre relaxing, friendly, not to spoil the mood any further, and gleefully replied to him in kind with a grin, "Or a curse!" We laughed with delight at the unrehearsed exchange.

Later, after dinner in another café, alone with Pierre, he confided: "Elisabeth comes from a sheltered background, Catholic. Father was a resistance hero. Imprisoned in concentration camps, including Dachau I think, multiple escapes. Now an important person in the conservative press. Strict. She rebelled. Broke with her family. Met up with a guy while still quite young, not even 20, an older fellow studying in one of the grand schools, Science Politique. His name is Lionel. People graduate from Science Po and go into leadership positions in high government circles. It is like one of your Ivy League schools. He is a good catch, from a conventional, bourgeois point of view."

"She was together with Lionel for years, but then they broke up, I don't know why. Later she met Jacques. They have been together for a time. Lionel tries to get her back from time to time but she refuses."

I offered, not to be outdone by this Lionel character, whoever he might be: "I went to an Ivy League school."

Pierre seemed amused. "Oh yes, which one?"

I replied, "Princeton."

He confirmed: "In New Jersey."

I nodded yes.

"So much the better for you," he concluded, with a smile. "You can pay for our drinks."

III

During that night, the Communist Party and the major trade unions - the Confédération Générale du Travail (CGT) and the Force Ouvrière (CGT-FO) called for a one day general strike and demonstration. One explosive issue was a headline in the right wing press calling Dani Cohn-Bendit a German Jew and demanding his expulsion from France.

Our groupe met and went to the staging point at Denfert-Rochereau to protest together. Cohn-Bendit was in front, as the head of the demonstration. We marched with countless others. All types of associations, unions, walks and ways of life met at different staging points across town, and by the time we got to Bastille, the various groups merged, and the lines stretched endlessly up the broad boulevard. Of the many slogans chanted that day, some called for the resignation of Prime Minister Pompidou, or denounced de Gaulle's use of police force, but the most prevalent was a defiant one proclaiming, "'We are all German Jews!" The line of marchers walked all the way up the Champs Elysee and to the Arc de Triomphe, which was a fair distance in all. When it was over the French news agency estimated was that more than a million people had participated.

The police stayed out of sight.

By way of reconciliation, the government released previously detained protesters en masse, and announced that the Sorbonne would reopen for normal classes.

But the Sorbonne again was invaded and occupied by rebellious students, not content with promised lukewarm reforms. Rumors of strikes became more not less frequent.

I strolled down to Jussieu. The place had been also reoccupied by demonstrators, like the Sorbonne, and was again bustling with people knocking themselves out to bring the word to others. I climbed the stairs to the second floor auditorium and the same pair was still talking to themselves across an empty littered room, as though I had never left. They were tireless.

FRIC: "Office workers, factory workers, faculty workers, you are all exploited. You are all deprived of a full and meaningful life by an economic system that holds you like an octopus in its tentacles.

It governs you when you wake. It controls you when you commute. It stifles you in the workplace. It directs you where to eat, what to consume, with whom to associate, it even controls your dreams. It fuels worthless ambitions, greed, lust for power. It dehumanizes. It creates atrocities like Vietnam, and before it, Algeria. Colonialism, racism are its offspring.

"Awake, Awake! The working class is rising up. It will liberate you from this monster.

"Long live the revolution!"

FRAC: "Sister comrades. Throw off the bourgeois yoke of subjugation to the ruling class of men. Realize your potential. Free your body from the constraints of the anti-abortionists, the anti-feminists, the misogynists. Don't settle for a second-class role as an underpaid worker relegated to the inferior jobs or a housewife whose role is to cook and clean and then be cheated upon by alienated husbands with mistresses as your reward.

"Join the revolution!"

You had to hand it to them. They didn't do much for me, kind of like a worn opening   Las Vegas act, but little did I know what would come next.

Chapter Four: Worker Student Commission

MAY 13-31, 1968

I

As I crossed the Place de la Contrescarpe the next morning, I spotted a headline in a kiosk that a sit-down strike in the city of Nantes had begun. I bought a paper. Metal workers had occupied their airplane factory and locked management in their offices. The official union had been side-stepped. It was a wildcat strike.

Hearing the news from official sources and not just the rumor mill generated electricity around the Quarter.

I went down to the Jussieu faculty and got there just in time to see two rough looking guys start climbing the stairs to the second floor in search of the "Worker Student Commission". I went about my business and checked the second floor lecture hall a couple of hours later. The two fellows that I called Fric and Frac were huddled with the new guys. I was told by someone else in the room that they were from the Renault factory at Boulogne-Billancourt, outside of Paris, come to check things out.

I scooted down to the Jussieu faculty asap the very next morning. The Renault factory had gone on a wildcat strike the same night after the two guys returned from the faculty.

Now two other rough looking guys were there in the company of the original two from the day before, again huddled with Fric and Frac in the large second floor lecture hall. I was told that the new guys were from the Peugot factory, brought by the first two guys from Renault.

The next day the headlines announced that the Peugot factory was on strike. This was front page stuff.

I went back down to the faculty at Jussieu again and climbed the stairs to the second floor auditorium. The trash was gone. There were small groups of people, talking. I caught snatches of conversation. Increasing numbers of rank and file members of unions were siding with the movement against the wishes and orders of their own leadership. Fric and Frac were now sprinkled in with other people, mingling. A woman went to the front of the hall and asked for attention.

She was taking a roll-call of the worker organizations present in the hall. The list was long considering this was only the second or third day of the strikes.

That night the word came that actors had occupied the National Theater and declared it a place for national debate on the role of the performing arts in the Revolution.

We walked over as a group later that night to see for ourselves, Jacques, Elisabeth, Maurice, crazy Pete, Pierre, a couple that I had not met before and myself. It was a long walk, across the river and a ways beyond that. It took almost an hour and a half one way. I chatted with the couple to whom I had just been introduced. The guy's name was Martin. He was of medium height and build with bushy black hair. I thought I detected an accent.

"South African," he said, switching to English. "You?"

"American," I replied.

"Thought maybe so," he commented.

"What brings you to France?" I asked.

He turned to his girlfriend and thoughtfully asked if it was okay with her to continue speaking English, which might exclude her.

"Go ahead," she said in heavily accented school English, gesturing. "I can maybe keep up."

In response as to why he was in France, he replied, "I had been active in a student organization protesting apartheid back home. My family bought me a ticket and got me out just in time, just before the cops came to get me. I have been a student here ever since."

"For how long?" I asked.

"Since last summer. Met Marie-Jeanne here a short time after I arrived and we have been together ever since."

Marie-Jeanne was decidedly French, with a fresh co-ed appearance, a long pony tail, and demure, gentle manner, though I got the distinct impression she could speak up forcibly for what she believed as necessary.

As we arrived people milled about, coming and going, while some people, presumably actors, did improvised skits or talked in groups among themselves on a stage. A lot of people were squeezed in.

Jacques mingled, talked with some people, and reported to us, "There are a couple of people I need to see, but unfortunately they are not around. Everybody seen enough?" No one objected, and so we turned around as a group and walked all the way back.

I had noticed Elisabeth did not walk next to Jacques on the way over, which continued on the way back. I wound up walking beside him.

"So, you attended school in Switzerland?" I asked, to make conversation, taking a cigarette and offering him one. He took it and I gave him a light.

"So you are smoking *Gaulloise*, now," he observed. "Good choice. They say the black tobacco in *Gaulloise* is better for you. Doesn't cut your wind as much as U.S. style tobacco, which we call blonde."

"I switched because I prefer the taste."

We smoked in silence for a moment.

"To answer your question," he began, "I did attend school in Switzerland, in Lausanne. Have you been there?"

I had not.

"It is beautiful, with a lake by the same name. You should go there if you get a chance. I can give you the name of some delightfully crazy people to look up."

"I may take you up on that," I replied. "Why Switzerland?"

"I was unwilling to serve in the military during the Algerian war. I refused to fight a war of colonial imperialism, like you and Vietnam. So I left France and went to Switzerland, among other places."

"But you came back," I observed.

"Evidently," he replied.

We continued in silence for a moment.

"I have a confession," I began. "I have permission of the authorities that decide about military service to be here in France. I proposed a study program to them that had national security importance, arguably. They gave me a deferment. I am not really in all that much of a bind. More the reverse."

"But will you be done with military service upon your return?" he asked, as we strolled, taking a puff.

"No, not quite."

"Then I don't see much difference in the situations, really," he said. "Besides, so much the better for you if it works out to your liking and you don't get called up to serve. It is not much fun to have to leave everything you know, no matter how much one may like to travel and experience new places."

"What did you do in Switzerland besides study?" I asked, making conversation again.

"I got involved in politics." No surprise there. "I fell in with a group of Leninists. That was an education. I came back inoculated against the virus the dictatorship of the proletariat, as a result of certain personal experiences."

He did not elaborate.

"What do you study now?" I asked. It felt like pulling teeth, getting Jacques to open up.

"I am doing personal research on some historical figures. I work in a bookstore that is very interesting with like-minded friends. I am enrolled in school and take some courses, but that is not my principal focus."

We continued in silence, and I fell back with the others.

Elizabeth's step was lively, almost jaunty, and she had a relaxed confident look on her face.

"You seem in good form," I commented, as we fell in step together.

She turned to me and said brightly, "I am, thank you. For once I know who I am and why I am here."

And then she paused, as though suddenly remembering something lost or forgotten, and said, with a far-away look in her eye, "I think."

II

Each day, the number of attendees in the second floor hall of the Jussieu faculty grew larger. It seems as one factory went on strike, someone among the strikers had a contact with someone else in a non-striking establishment, maybe as a friend, family member, soccer teammate, former workmate, or habitué of the same neighborhood café.

A call would be made or a personal visit paid. They would talk among themselves. Someone would contact someone else. And so on.

As though magically, an independent network of cooperating workers taking common aim at their unions, their employers, and the government sprang into existence, fed by revolutionary fervor. The strikes were wildcat, in the sense that they were conceived and initiated outside the official union leadership, but they were often coordinated, guided and assisted by the second floor University participants, who took decisions by a majority vote of those present at any given moment. And what made these strikes different from ones I had seen in films or read about, workers often remained in the factories, occupying them and imprisoning management in their own offices, and did not limit their activities to just picketing out in front.

Each day representatives from further and further away arrived to take part, in one case, as far away as Alsace-Lorraine, on the German border.

Outside, the newspapers could talk of nothing else except the revolution. "Métro, boulot, dodo" (subway, job, sleep) had become a common chant in street demonstrations, and it was adopted as the analytic framework for an in-depth article in an establishment paper *"Le Monde"* about the ills of modern society, with revolutionary sentiment as a symptom if not a solution. Endless news programs treated one aspect or another of the movement on a daily basis. It became all-encompassing. You couldn't escape it, if you had wanted to.

A number of cafés, restaurants and businesses in the Latin Quarter closed and shuttered during this time, fearing the worst. In their place, food stalls and mobile business sprang up in the streets, likely illegal, but the police were avoiding a presence for the time being in the Quarter, so carts even sometimes blocked traffic. I spent most of the time navigating through it, sometimes with friends, sometimes not, sleeping little, taking it all in, on the prowl. It went on sometimes day and night, a seeming perennial block party that spanned many blocks, where there was always something to see or hear.

Walking around one night, Pierre remarked: "It is, like you Americans, say a 'hoppening'", opening his arms theatrically as he pronounced the English word with exaggerated difficulty, for his own amusement and delight.

A cranked up stereo blared a pop song from an open second story window.

We stopped at a food cart and, standing on a sidewalk, ate a dinner of steak and fries prepared on the spot over a propane stove. It was good.

Suddenly a small group of people marched past us, cross-dressers, with banners proclaiming equal rights for homosexuals, pounding on tambourines. We watched, dumbfounded, along with other astonished bystanders.

Apparently no one had ever seen anything like it before.

After they passed, Pierre made a crude gesture for my benefit, inserting and withdrawing the forefinger of one hand repeatedly into a circle of his thumb and forefinger of the other. "I wish them good luck, but I don't see how people can propagate otherwise." He shrugged his shoulders as he popped a fry into his mouth. "It's a no-brainer."

III

In the middle of this whirlwind of activity, I received a letter from a girl in the States who was arriving in Amsterdam and wondered if I could meet her. We had had a lot of fun together, just before I had left for Europe.

I had recently purchased a car from a departing student for next to nothing that seemed to run just fine. I parked it on the streets and moved it periodically to prevent it from being towed away. But I had not filled it up since I had bought it, the gas refineries were on strike in sympathy with the students, and gasoline was being rationed through the petrol stations only to doctors, so I still had no sure way of getting to Amsterdam.

I discovered that gasoline was still being produced by the striking workers in their facilities and delivered directly from the refineries to the faculty at Jussieu. A lot of it was stored on the top floor, for use in private vehicles performing tasks for the Revolution, or ultimately as Molotov cocktails, if it came to that.

I ran into Jacques in the faculty and approached him with my dilemma. He was amused, and sympathetic. He motioned with a jerk of the head for me to follow. We climbed stairs to the roof. He signaled me to wait there. The night was cool and the view of the city from the faculty's roof outstanding. Jacques returned with an older man. Jacques explained my plight. "An affair of the heart" is how he put it. An indulgent smile broke out across the older man's face. "Wait here," he gestured. He came back with a jerry can of gas. "Should easily get you as far as Belgium. Just bring the can back later."

I left in the early morning. The streets were bereft of vehicles. I turned onto the multi-lane highway headed north. Not a car or truck could be seen in either direction, all the way from Paris to the Belgian border. It was like being in a spooky, post-apocalyptic movie.

I reached Amsterdam in the afternoon, just in time to meet the airplane. She looked lovely and inviting, but I knew in an instant it was all wrong. We spent the night together, but the events in Paris kept pulling me back like a magnet. It was an awkward encounter. In the morning, I couldn't see myself playing tourist with her, relaxing at a shore, idling pleasant time away. It all seemed so trivial compared to what was going on in France. I was wired and ready for more action. I missed the groupe already. I made my lame excuses, apologized, turned the car around, and headed straight back to Paris.

I ran into Jacques soon after my return.

"Back so soon?" he exclaimed. "Did it not go well?"

"I found that I couldn't vacation right now, not with everything going on here. She pulled me back."

"Who did?" asked Jacques.

"That bitch goddess the Revolution, miserable thing that she is."

"You are engaged in the struggle, like us, like me. Maybe it was worth the trip to find that out," he replied in a comradely way.

I wasn't so sure. Perhaps it was more like being a moth drawn to the flames.

IV

It seemed like I had been going up and down the stairs to the second floor lecture hall at Jussieu for half of my life, though it had been only a little over a week since the strikes had begun.

I must becoming an adrenaline addict, I thought, pulling out one last cigarette for a quick smoke before going back in. I nodded to a few folks in the corridor whose faces were becoming familiar to me, though we may never have actually met or talked.

The same discussion was going on about helping workers at the Renault factory that had been in progress when I took the last break to stretch my legs. There had to be other things going on in the world. Apparently things had gotten sticky for the strikers at Renault after the government, management and union officials had ganged up on the workers, and people were trying to figure how best to help.

A man zoomed by me breathlessly, burst into the hall and got people's attention. He announced, "The unions are telling the Métro workers that other stations are returning from the strike but it is a lie. We need to get the word out, before more strikers are tricked into returning to work."

"The bastards!" someone called out.

Another man raised his hand. "Hey-ho", he signaled. "Did you contact Roger? He's handling that."

"Who is Roger?" asked the first. The second man approached. They conferred.

"We need a car to get to Roger." The phones were not getting through, the workers in the telecommunications services were on strike too. "Roger can get the word out to the right people, if we act quickly."

"Who has a car, anyone have a car?"

A hand went up. "I do, but it needs gas."

"Who can get him gas?"

Two hands shot up. "Follow them," said the person who was leading the assembly. They exited quickly.

The discussion returned to how best to assist the strikers at the Renault factory. I began fidgeting in my seat, wondering if I shouldn't have offered to go help Roger in my own car.

I had been at it too long. I needed a real break. I gave up my seat to someone else.

Before I could get gracefully out the door, another speaker was recognized. He was tall, mid-forty-ish, stocky, dark hair. He hesitated, began, stuttered, began again.

"Do not be shy or afraid," the woman who was leading the discussion said, encouragingly. "You are among friends."

"I am from the North. The guys want strike." (His accent was thick, foreign. I could not place it.) "We immigrants are in … it is difficult. We are foreign. I am in favor. But many of my compatriots are not. Afraid. Do not want expelled."

"How can we help?" asked the moderator.

"Can get someone to come speak, please?"

A voice called out. "We need to adopt a platform for the immigrant workers!"

Hear, hear, came a murmur from the crowd.

"And immigrant students!" called out another.

To her credit the moderator ignored the fact that neither speaker had been recognized by her.

"Is there any other immigrant group we need to address?" she asked.

Hearing no response, she motioned to the two people who have just spoken and the immigrant worker, "Can you get together and come up with something for the rest of us to consider? Anyone else have something to contribute? Please go with them. Is there a room available? Yes? The number?"

Then, she asked, "What country are you from?"

"Portugal," he replied.

"Anyone speak Portuguese?" she inquired of the assembly.

A woman raised her hand.

"Can you go with them and help translate?"asked the moderator.

As they left the room, the assembly moved on to another subject.

My cue to exit stage left, I told myself. I scooted out too.

V

I bought more smokes and a newspaper in a tabac and read it standing up in the street. It reported that a total of ten million workers were now on strike, which was roughly a third of the work force of the entire country. It concluded that none of the strikes had been initiated by the union leadership. The Métro, telephones, industrial refineries were all shut down. The airlines and airports were affected as well. Even television was off the air.

The Government was switching tactics. With the overt support of management (and covert of the unions, according to the article), it treated the grievances as economic, to be solved practically by higher wages, and not existential, which was fundamentally disruptive to the existing order.

The article continued that a 35% increase in the minimum wage, a 7% wage increase for other workers, and compensation at half-time of normal pay for the workers who had gone on strike was being negotiated.

I sat down on a public bench and went through the paper more carefully. Events were coming to a head at lightning speed.

The Government was proceeding to finalize a formal agreement, called the Grenelle accords to embody the terms.

As I sat reading, Martine, the server from the student restaurant, strolled up. She wore her hip length boots, close-fitting jeans and a sweater. She looked stunning in an understated way. She greeted me in a friendly fashion.

I folded up the paper.

"What are you up to?" she asked. We shook hands and kissed each other on the cheek with a peck, French-style.

"Overwhelmed by all this revolutionary talk and action," I replied, "And you?"

"On my way to Île de la Cité. You do look a little frazzled," she commented. "How about walking over there with me? Might do you some good and I could use the company."

It wasn't far, not more than a half mile or so away.

"Deal."

As we strolled down towards the Seine, I commented, "I guess there is no more work in the student restaurant. How are you managing?"

"I'm doing fine," she replied, her eyes and smile flashing, "thanks."

"Let me ask you, as a member of the working class, how do you feel about all of this?"

"I hope it succeeds," she replied carefully, so as not to offend. "I wish them -- you all -- luck."

"But you don't feel part of it? It doesn't grab you? Suck you in?"

"Definitely not," she concluded after a moment's reflection, smiling happily. "Not my bag. Maybe I'm just not as intense as the rest of you."

"Should I try to convince you?" I asked.

"Don't waste your breath," she assured me. "It wouldn't be the first time someone has tried."

She shot me a look. "But what about you? Are you really a revolutionary that you would convince me of the merits of your cause? Or is this something you are trying on for size, like a new brand of cigarettes?"

I shrugged, not knowing how to respond.

"So what errand are you on?" I asked, changing the subject.

She looked at me sideways. "My stash is getting low."

"They sell it on the Île de la Cité, in the center of town, just like that?" I asked.

"Watch and learn," she replied with a smile, taking my arm in hers.

The Île de la Cité is an island in the middle of the Seine, between the left and right banks where the courts and other government buildings are located, including the central office of the Paris prefecture of police. It is in the heart of ancient Paris. Notre-Dame sits on one part of it. I couldn't believe that stuff was sold openly there.

We crossed the bridge and Martine led me down some stone stairs to the river level. We strolled along the Quai, towards the part of the island that was farthest away from Île St. Louis, a nearby companion island that also is situated in the river Seine between the two banks.

People were lounging along the Quai. Several wore white Muslim head coverings. We went to a little park at the extreme tip of the island. Martine proceeded directly to one of the Muslim men. She exchanged greetings with him and introduced me as a friend. The man shook my hand without getting up as we exchanged greetings in French.

He took out some rolling papers, licked the glued portion of one, affixed the papers together at an odd angle, rolled the combined papers into a cone, and put a tightly coiled narrow cardboard strip in the cone's tip as a filter. Then he filled the cone with a mixture of tobacco and crumbled hashish.

"It is called a shalem," said Martine. "It is how they smoke it in North Africa."

"Try it," he offered, extending it to me.

I refused politely with a hand gesture. He handed to Martine who lit it.

"Not bad," she said after a moment. "How much?"

They settled on the price. The transaction was completed.

The shalem was still going. We sat down on a bench.

"Want to try some?" she offered, her hand prudently cupping the device to hide it from view.

"Nah, thanks," I said.

"I thought that getting high is all that college students did in California," she teased. "Streets paved in green instead of gold."

"I never did," I replied.

"Never?" she asked in disbelief.

I shook my head in confirmation.

"Then you must try it now," she said decisively. "When else will you get the chance?"

I hesitated. What the hell, I thought. I took the cone from her.

I inhaled deeply and took a second drag.

"Go easy," she counseled. "Wait before you take any more. It can take time before you feel it. You don't want to overdo it."

After a few minutes, I started to feel the effects. I got a little light-headed, and I could feel my limbs relax. The more we sat there, the more I liked just sitting.

We quietly watched the play of light on the water, and the patterns of the sparkles. The breeze was cool. It was pleasant in the shade.

"Do you like Arabic food?" she asked. "I know a great place."

I started to reach for my wallet, to see if I had money.

"It's cheap, don't worry. It'll be my treat."

I was about to ask if she was sure, but she had already stood up and was ready to get going. She got rid of the remains of the shalem in the river by crumbling it first, discretely.

What the hell, I thought to myself. Why not?

We took the Métro. The thought fleetingly crossed my mind that Roger must not have gotten through to the striking Métro workers yet, or maybe the guys from the Worker Student Commission couldn't find him.

There weren't many unoccupied seats in the subway car, so I made sure she got one, while I stood. A man standing nearby me reeked of garlic. The smell was overpowering, but it did not occur to me to move away.

The restaurant was in a part of town I had never visited. There were crowded small streets and spicy scents, a stark contrast to the shuttered stores of the Latin Quarter.

The restaurant was tiny, scarcely more than a couple of tables, but it was an off-hour.

The patrons greeted Martine warmly. She introduced me. The food took a while, but it was delicious when it finally came.

I felt peaceful. I ate the couscous leisurely, enjoying the taste.

Martine talked about Martinique, where she came from, her infant daughter, her own mother, and life in the apartment that they all shared. The grandmother took care of the baby when Martine worked or took a day to herself. She loved the child, clearly.

After the meal we strolled contentedly, sometimes talking, sometimes not.

Before we knew it, it was dusk.

She asked for a cigarette and I gave her one. I lit it. We faced each other.

She inquired softly, turning her shoulder slightly in a sensual way, with a come-hither look in her eyes, "How close is your place?"

"Not far," I assured her, desire stirring.

We ambled, occasionally brushing lightly against each other, enjoying the subtle touch, chatting amiably, anticipation building.

When we got to my flat, I showed her a little record player that I had picked up in the flea market on my wanderings. The switches and back plate were legended in Cyrillic characters.

"How peculiar, I wonder what country it comes from," she remarked. "Do you have any records?"

"One."

I pulled out a vinyl record in fairly decent condition that I had found at Shakespeare and Company, an American bookstore in Paris. It included Judy Collin's rendition of Leonard Cohen's *Suzanne*.

I put it on for her and poured two glasses of red wine.

She tasted. "Not too bad. Not quite disgusting." She laughed. "So, what is she singing about?"

"It's complicated, but here," I lifted a finger in anticipation of the verse and then sang along to the words in English, "I touched her perfect body with my mind."

"What does that mean?"

To remain true to the mores of that era, of what happened next, I must respectfully demure.

She left in the very early morning.

I lay atop the crumpled bedcovers, dozing to the sounds of the wakening city through the half-opened window.

I fell into a dream, then awoke with a start. How long had I been asleep? Already the dream was slipping from me.

It took place in my father's house, in Arizona. He and my step-mother were preparing for a backyard home wedding. Their substantial home was in a lovely setting, replete with swimming pool, garden, surrounding desert, and mountain views. They actually did weddings like this for friends from time to time. My step-mother had been licensed to perform marriages. She was to officiate but at the last minute the couple had informed her by telephone that a Catholic priest was going to perform the ceremony instead. She was furious, and stormed about the house, attacking the bride and groom as deluded fools who had been duped by religion, which was the opiate of the masses, and threatening to cancel the affair. (Her words. She was in fact an avowed Communist and atheist). I had asked a question challenging her harsh condemnation of the couple, which had incited her further and directed her fury against me. (It was a scene that had in fact played out in real life before).

I still felt the anger and resentment towards her for demanding blind allegiance to her doctrinaire views and disrespecting my freedom to think for myself.

The dream had ended with my father seated across from me at the kitchen table, a happy smile on his face and a twinkle in his eye.

"You see," he explained in the dream, "You do a thing with your whole heart for as long as it is good, then move on."

Did this relate to Martine's question about my revolutionary commitment? It had bothered me that I had had no ready answer for her at the time.

Something in my father's words comforted me, as permission to be just as I was being in the face of the events that were playing themselves out.

But influencing the destinies of others perhaps was a different matter. I vowed to be more attentive in the future to the possible impact on others.

I only emerged late that afternoon. I bought a paper and coffee. I scanned the news. Rank and file strikers had unanimously rejected the Grenelle accords. Someone had set fire to the stock market. President de Gaulle had gone into hiding, resurfaced, and just pardoned two former right wing generals formerly convicted and serving time for excesses during the Algerian insurgency a decade earlier. Tanks had been spotted along the highways surrounding the outskirts of Paris.

Can't take a day off without everything going to pieces, I joked to myself darkly, as I headed up to the Place de la Contrescarpe.

Nothing was open so I wound up eating dinner with Pierre and Elisabeth in the small kitchen of their apartment. It was a simple meal of some cheese ends, a bit of pate, semi-fresh bread, and wine.

"So what do you make of all of this?" asked Pierre.

"Never seen anything like it in my life. I'm speechless." I replied honestly.

"Come, let's finish up. Some right wing generals have offered machine guns to the students. There is a debate tonight whether or not to accept the offer. It could be crucial to what happens next."

So back we went to the faculty of Jussieu and climbed the stairs once again to the second floor.

The debate was already in full swing. A young woman was addressing the assembly from down front, in a state of distress.

"What do you mean 'too dangerous'? Did not you not know it would inevitably come to this? A show of force? What were you thinking? Of course blood must be shed for the Revolution. The existing order will not give up its privileges without a fight to the finish."

"But the barrels of the guns could be welded shut. It's a set-up," replied a man next to her, leaning against a wall. "A justification for gunning us down like rats, powerless to defend ourselves."

"Hey, how do we know there aren't police informants in the hall? Shouldn't this be discussed privately?" shouted out someone.

"There have likely been informants in the hall since the beginning," replied the young woman peevishly. "Why are you bringing that up now?" And then accusingly, "What are you up to? What are you trying to pull?"

He did not respond.

She addressed the hall, impassioned. "We have come so far. This is the end of the beginning. Now comes the real Revolution. We need to be armed. They will be, and they are coming soon!" she cried out.

"You exaggerate", muttered someone, loudly enough to be heard.

"Do I?" she replied with fury. "Did you think that papa will save his precious little child in the end? That you will be able to go home and sleep in your childhood bed when this is over? Is that what you thought the Revolution was? A game to drop when you tired of it or it got too scary?"

The hall fell quiet.

"Cowards! Cowards!" she shouted, then exited the room, fuming, on the verge of tears.

After a moment's silence, the young man who had been leaning against the wall stood erect and asked, "Shall we take a vote? All those in favor of accepting the guns, raise your hand."

There were a number of raised hands. Surprising to me, most of those came from women.

"The nays have it."

It wasn't even close.

Pierre, Elisabeth and I found a café open on the way back from the faculty.

"You did not vote," observed Elisabeth. "Could you not decide?"

"It wasn't my place," I said. "I'll be returning home shortly. I won't be here to face the consequences. It would not be right."

"Oh, whatever happens will happen before you depart, of that I am sure," said Pierre confidently.

"Don't you see that everyone's actions matter?" said Elisabeth. "Shit, either we are all working for the revolution or not."

"I am not in favor of violence," I said.

"Who is?" she replied. "But what of the quiet violence of daily life for those without work or bread? And of the deadly violence required to perpetuate the system? Don't you see, one must remain engaged, vigilant?"

"I would have voted against it," I said quietly. "Abstaining is the same thing."

"Not in such matters," she replied with passion. "Every voice adds to every other voice. The whole exceeds the sum. Stand up and be counted; otherwise we let each other down. But do as you will," she concluded coldly, in a tone of finality and with a deprecatory wave of the hand, suddenly indifferent.

Chapter Five: Aftermath

JUNE 1-AUGUST 24, 1968

I

With the army firmly behind him, De Gaulle went on the radio to announce new legislative elections. A right wing counter-demonstration took place along the Champs-Élysées a day or two later, which bolstered the Government, according to the press. De Gaulle's own party won a landslide victory in the elections that were held the next month. The strikes collapsed; the students were evicted from the faculties, which soon reopened for normal classes. Student organizations were banned. Cohn-Bendit was expelled from the country. It was over almost as quickly as it had begun.

With the reopening of the Faculty of Law where I was still enrolled, I decided to take the final exams, even though I had not opened a book or attended a class for many months. I locked myself in my room for three days and nights, emerging only for food and smokes.

Jacques gave me pointers. "Each exam or paper in the French school system should contain two main points, or parts. Then these are then subdivided into sub-parts, ideally each consisting of two each as well, and so on."

I resurrected my old study habits. I took both written and oral exams, lasting several days.

Afterwards, I decided to take some time away from Paris. I had remained in contact with Martin, the South African. He told me that he and his girlfriend were moving away from Paris. They were re-locating to Corsica, to live and work in a small artist community. He invited me to visit.

I still owned the car, so I took a road trip in it south to Nice, to catch the ferry to Corsica. His girlfriend's family lived there. They welcomed me warmly, treated me to a fine meal, and instructed me about the ferry. I left my car on the mainland with them.

The crossing took all night. The weather was clear and mild. I slept on a lounge chair under the stars. There was no one else on deck. In the morning I took a bus from the port into the nearby hills, to a tiny village, Palasca, where the community, Cine Arte, was located. I arrived at midday.

They were camped out in a chateau that was partially in ruins.

"We're going to restore it bit by bit," explained Martin. There were others too. They worked and slept in the various rooms, some of which lacked complete walls.

I wondered if it was safe, but kept the concern to myself.

They showed me to a room with a bed and old-style shuttered windows. Traces of ancient wallpaper remained. The walls and ceiling seemed intact.

"It was the master bed-room," said Martin.

"I am honored," I said.

"Someone was supposedly murdered in it," replied Martin good naturedly, "a long time ago. Let us know if you encounter any ghosts."

"Murdered in the very same bed?" I asked.

"Maybe not," he replied with a grin.

The chateau was situated slightly above the village, with a commanding view of the hills, and not far away, the beach and the ocean, where I spent a lot of time.

There were a couple of artists in residence. One, Guy, was a short wiry oil painter from Bordeaux, with shoulder length dark hair and Mediterranean complexion. He was young, and very talented.

Another, a heavy-set fair-skinned youth from Paris, was a sculptor. He did not talk much.

I spent a relaxing week hanging out with them, then returned to the mainland and drove back to Paris.

Afterwards, I resumed my life in the Quarter. I found some of the groupe at Chez Sadoul. They were discussing the news that isolated remnants of strikers were still holding out in some localities, with immigrant workers often the last to submit, but the police were evicting them all steadily from the factories.

The mood was bleak.

"We must redouble the resistance," argued Suleiman. "Find arms. Attack."

Finding no takers, he said to the table at large: "What is wrong with you? Snap out of it. This is just the beginning. This is how it works with the dialectic. One step backwards, two steps forward."

His persistent tone did not help and soon the table was empty except for him and me. "And you," he said to me, "you are coming to the meeting with me."

"What meeting?" I asked with surprise.

"What difference what meeting it is?" he snarled, suddenly looming over me. I stood up too.

He punched me in the shoulder, hard.

"That is an order, comrade, not an invitation."

I looked at him, disbelieving.

"I don't think so, pal," I said as I walked out of the café without looking back.

II

I ran into Elisabeth, in the street. I had not seen her in a while. The meeting was a little awkward.

"Can I speak with you?" she asked.

"Sure," I replied. "Let me walk with you."

"I shouldn't have spoken to you in the way that I did on the night of the meeting," she offered a little sheepishly, "after the vote was taken. I was too harsh. I apologize."

"Thank you," I said, "but there is no need."

"What is freedom anyway if you can't exercise it freely?" she joked, smiling easily again.

We chatted as we walked. She told me that she had gone to Czechoslovakia with Jacques and a few others to witness the Prague Spring for themselves first hand; the mood had been free and jubilant, much like that in France though more nationalistic and in some ways (but not all), less ideological. The threats of the Soviets seemed much more dangerous than those of the government in France, but she added, one could not always properly assess these things in the moment. I told her about my trip to Corsica.

We finally reached her building.

"Well, here we are", I said awkwardly.

"Still friends?" she asked, earnestly extending a hand to shake on it.

I took her extended right hand in my left one, and with it I drew her towards me. Our gaze met. I kissed her full on the lips.

We were in full view in the narrow street but it was Paris after all, so I figured what the hell. I'd had been wanting to do that for such a long time.

She pulled back, startled a little by my forwardness, and perhaps her own reaction.

She seemed to weigh the experience for a brief instant, then leaned forward and kissed me experimentally back. We hung there in space. She pulled back again and studied me as though seeing me for the first time.

We kissed again. I felt heat emanate from her. I became intoxicated. Passion rose from us mutually.

She was flushed, eyes bright. "Come," she said. She grabbed my hand, hurrying. I matched her gait and mood. She laughed mischievously. We rushed up the stairs, hand in hand, nearly colliding with an old lady coming down, avoiding her indignant glare, entered the apartment and her bedroom, shucked off our clothes and lay in each other's arms on the bedcovers, just regarding each other, still for a moment, unmoving, under each other's spell.

Then she pulled me slowly and gently to her, reaching for me, guidingly, her eyes reflecting blue depths.

Later, after a brief nap, she murmured sleepily, as though in response to my unspoken thought: "The shower is at the end of the corridor past Pierre's bedroom."

And later still:

"When will I see you again?" I asked as I was leaving.

"Come back tonight?" she asked.

I nodded in agreement.

We spent the better part of the next weeks in each other's company, together at night and sometimes during parts of the day, as our schedules permitted.

We had no disagreements, no quarrels.

"We seem to be compatible," I remarked one night.

She said. "Because we have no past or future. No baggage, no hopes or fears. No pressure. You are leaving and I am staying.

That is all there is. Only here and now. This is an … interlude. To be enjoyed. For itself. Like a gift."

I added, after a moment of reflection. "I think it is because I see you and you see me, like children at play."

"Playing at what?" she asked with mock innocence, then rolled towards me and tousled my hair, like a child's. "Mmm?"

One night, after dinner in a local restaurant we both liked, Elisabeth suggested we take coffee in a café with which I was unfamiliar. I agreed.

It was a place that I had never frequented. As we entered, a man opened the glass door for us. It opened inward. Elisabeth went first. The man said elegantly to me, "I am the doorman," bowing slightly. He was in street clothes, so it was obvious he was not really a doorman.

I thanked him and attempting to be light and agreeable in return, I said something like "it is a noble profession."

He then socked me one good in the jaw. I didn't even see it coming. I stumbled backward, momentarily stunned, uttered a curse in English, and wound up out in the street, fumbling for my glasses, wondering what had just happened.

It took a little while, but then Elisabeth came rushing out. I started to go back in but she restrained me.

"Don't," she said. "He has friends in there. They are waiting for you. They intend to beat you up if you go inside."

"Why?" I asked. "I don't even know him."

"He is a Communist. So are his friends. They call you 'the American,' but as an ugly reference, not like we do. He is jealous, that is all."

"Wait, is he a friend of Suleiman?" I asked.

"No, I am sure not. Please just keep walking. Here, let me take a look at that." She examined my jaw. "You'll live. Let's get some ice for it."

A few days later I told Pierre about the incident, still puzzled by it.

"Where is this café?" he asked. I described the location and the decor.

"Was this man who struck you tall?" he asked suddenly.

"Yes, very tall. His punched down at me."

"Aha," he said, thinking. "Elisabeth used to meet Lionel from time to time in a café, but I don't know which one," he said finally. "Lionel is tall."

"Hair?" I asked.

We looked at each other.

"Dark, very curly" he replied.

"I think I was had," I said finally.

He did not want to take sides. "It is possible," was all that he allowed.

"What is his last name, in case I ever meet up with him again?"

He told me.

I shook my head, then started to laugh.

"She's right. He is jealous, if it was Lionel. And what the heck, he has every right to be, I am still with the girl, and he is not. Best revenge there can be."

He was relieved I was not angry, and actually he thought it was pretty humorous too, viewed in that light.

In truth, I had found the incident troubling, but I was unwilling to let it spoil our time together. If she had brought me to the café to make Lionel jealous, as I suspected, I think she never intended harm to befall me. I felt certain that nothing like would happen again.

And yet I wondered if the incident revealed an aspect of our relationship that neither of us had considered or discussed before. For her, perhaps our time together was not only an expression of a professed free-spiritedness but perhaps also a salve and temporary refuge against the revolution's failure and its implied broken promise to free her from the trappings of an unfulfilled, inauthentic life, which now seemed all but inevitable to her.

It wasn't a particularly pretty or complimentary thought, but if she had unresolved feelings, she could and probably would take care of them after I was gone.

I decided to put it out of my mind. I was still okay with the way things were between us.

III

I got back my exam results which were marked with a notation "mention bien".

I asked Elisabeth what it meant. "It is a notable achievement. Better than most other exams. High end of the scores."

"Too bad it doesn't confer a degree without writing a thesis but I don't think I will return just for that."

"Why did you take the exams then? As insurance?" She asked.

"Against what?"

"You still have the threat of military service over you when you go back? No?"

"Yes. For at least six more months."

"If you have to leave your country in order not to serve in the Vietnam War, will you do it, really?"

"Certainly." I meant it.

"Maybe then you will want to return to write the thesis and get the degree. You might even be able to get your scholarship back, at least the French portion of it. The exam results could come in handy."

"That might work. Thanks."

She added, "You know you have friends here, if it comes to that."

I still had one road trip to take before the year was up. I had begun corresponding with an official in the Communications Satellite Corporation in Washington, D.C., hoping to land a job there based on my credentials in satellite communications both from my last year in law school and the current year in France, meager as my studies in Paris had actually been. I was hoping to work there in the off-chance event I would not be drafted into military service. The response from the Comsat official had been encouraging. There was a conference to be held on international cooperation in Munich in June. Comsat was sponsoring it. He invited me to attend. The conference included a special performance and reception at the Munich Symphony.

I accepted.

Elisabeth told me of a quaint medieval village in eastern France that I absolutely had to visit on the way there; I think she remembered it fondly from childhood. I stopped briefly on the way out of France, but I was more interested in making time on the road than sight-seeing.

It was a long drive into Germany. I spent one night car camping in the Black Forest by myself, which was spooky. Otherwise most of Germany looked like parts of the American Midwest.

The Conference lasted a few days. I stayed at a cheap hotel. The manager was a young woman, a few years older than me. She took a shine to me. I invited her to accompany me to the symphony. It was an elegant affair. She dressed up for it. It was a treat. She in turn invited me into her bed. Just as I was starting to believe that everything bad I had learned and heard about Germany in the past was behind it, I was set straight.

On the last night, I went out into the area of the town near my hotel to eat. I saw a busy restaurant (my criterion for restaurant picking in an unfamiliar place) and sat alone at a table. Some workers spied me and enthusiastically motioned me over to join them. They were wearing the same kind of blue worker uniforms as their counterparts in France. At first, I felt right at home with them. I did not speak German and they did not speak English or French, so after the usual round of where I hailed from, one of the men pulled out some pictures and showed them to me. The first was of Adolph Hitler. "Gut," he said, jabbing the photo repeatedly and emphatically with his forefinger. I excused myself as if to go to the restroom, then went back to my table and ate alone.

As I came out of the restaurant, two men were arguing on the sidewalk. It quickly escalated into a fist fight. One of the men went over to a nearby construction site, grabbed a two by four and hit the other man over the head with it. Another man intervened to break up the fight. The two fighters ganged up on him. Police arrived. The two brawling men ran away. The Good Samaritan was stunned, unable to escape. The police arrested him and took him away.

I drove back to France the next morning. On the way, a field laborer spotted the F decal indicating I as from France on my bumper. He enthusiastically gave me the finger as I drove past.

I got to thinking that my previously unfavorable impression of Germany might have been correct.

IV

I returned to Paris. My year in France was coming to an end.

The time arrived to say good-bye, but the University Faculties had recessed for the summer, and the tourist season was in full swing. Many residents of Paris got out of town or went into hiding. The usual groupe was not around. I did find Maurice in Chez Sadoul, alone, reading a volume of Marx and Engels at a table, taking notes.

He asked, "Did you learn anything useful about the Revolution?"

"I think so," I said. "I am just not sure exactly what."

"When you figure it out, pass it on. In America. Or wherever you may be. That's how it works. We help each other. That's it in a nutshell."

I told him about Suleiman, and asked his opinion.

"It seems you were given a first-hand lesson from Suleiman about dictatorship of the proletariat, in miniature, in a manner of speaking. Maoists are bullies."

"And if they take control someday in a Revolution?"

"They won't. We are on to them. Never fear."

Somehow I was not completely reassured.

The only other casual acquaintance from the groupe I ran into before leaving was Crazy Pete. It was late in the day. He was with a group of people I did not know, sitting on the curb, unkempt, dirty and drunk, holding a large half-filled bottle of red wine. He began to get up to greet me, but fell back. He got up again, stupefied. He tried to talk to me, but overcome, he vomited a huge pool of stale wine and mucus into the street.

I offered to help, but he declined.

I waved good-bye to him and he returned a wave weakly back. "Hey, you want a chug?" he yelled drunkenly as an afterthought, holding up the bottle.

So this is how the revolution ends, I thought.

I said my goodbye's to Elisabeth in the morning. Our embrace was warm, I promised to call her when I landed (I did once) and I left, without looking back. That was our arrangement, and it suited us both.

I reserved some time before leaving for Pierre, the good friend to me he had been, and we shook hands sincerely at the end, mutually sorry for the separation that was to be.

Then I got on the Métro, and enjoyed a last ride, particularly when it emerged from underground and crossed over a bridge, affording me one last view of the city. As I boarded the TWA flight to New York, the stewardess handed me a complimentary English language newspaper. The lead story told of the latest body count and bombing raids over Vietnam. "Welcome, aboard", the stewardess intoned pleasantly. "Please prepare for departure."

Epilogue

Jacques Baynac became a published author of an influential book on leftist theory and action in the early 1970's, after a break with his friends from the bookstore over political doctrine, then established a notable career writing books and films on left wing subjects, including pivotal figures in the French resistance during World War II in the south of France, and in pre-revolutionary Russia. He is still active.

Pierre Arènes began a career as a French schoolteacher but found disrespect of literature in the classroom and his expected role as a disciplinarian difficult. He became very unhappy in the early years, during which time he discovered Buddhism. He continued teaching and deepening his knowledge of Buddhism, and in retirement became an active writer for the Revue d'Etudes Tibétaines, was respected by colleagues as an authority on Tibetan Buddhism and was a follower of Dagpo Rinpoche, a master. He fell ill on a trip to India and returned to France for treatment of cancer, where he died on May 17, 2012.

Martin Broomberg remained in Corsica and built a career as a blacksmith and metal-work artist. In 2008 his workshop burnt to the ground after he publicly denounced senseless violence directed against foreign visitors in the village where he had lived for 40 years. He rebuilt and continues his trade.

Lionel Jospin became the longest sitting Prime Minister of the Fifth Republic, from 1997 to 2002. He unsuccessfully ran for the Presidency of France as a Socialist in 1995 and 2002, barely losing in 1995 to Jacques Chirac, who coincidentally had been the negotiator of the Grenelle accords on behalf of the government in 1968.

Lionel was plagued in the final election of 2002 by accusations of hiding ties with the Troskyite OCI after joining the Socialist Party, in order to assist in a deliberate strategy of entrism (infiltration) into the cadres other parties.

Appendix: Chronology of Events

February 14, 1968	450 French students occupy the women's dormitory at the Faculty of Nanterre protesting separate dormitories for men and women mandated by governmental regulations, sparking protests at other campuses.
March 17, 1968	A major anti-Vietnam riot in Grosvernor Square in London leads to many injured and 200 arrested.
March 20, 1968	Students protesting the Vietnam War in front of the American Express in Paris are arrested by police and detained. One is a student from Nanterre
March 22, 1968	Students at Nanterre occupy the Administration building in support of the arrested Paris anti-Vietnam demonstrators. One faction (les Enragés) trashes the administration building and paints graffiti on the walls before leaving. The

	remaining students continue to protest the presence of plainclothes police on campus, the impersonality and automation of society, and arrests of students. Their group becomes known as the March 22 movement.
March 28, 1968	Nanterre faculty President closes the school for three days in response to repeated disruptions by the Enragés. A protest by 500 students is suppressed by riot police.
April 4, 1968	Dr. Martin Luther King is assassinated, sparking riots in the US.
April 11, 1968	An assassination attempt in Berlin of a leader of the West German anti-Vietnam student movement leads to sympathy protests by Nanterre demonstrators.
April 23, 1968	A student occupation spearheaded by the Students for a Democratic Society in New York City leads to closure of Columbia

	University. At issue were discovered links between Columbia and the U.S. Department of Defense, as well as University plans to build a segregated gymnasium in nearby Morningside Park.
April 30, 1968	Daniel Cohn Bendit and two other members of the March 22 movement are arrested for distributing leaflets at a Paris high school.
May 2, 1968	Students occupy the Administration building at Nanterre to show a film about the U.S. Black Panthers but are ejected. They retreat to an auditorium and eject the professor. The dean of Nanterre suspends all classes at Nanterre.
May 3, 1968	The March 22 movement organizes a March on the Sorbonne faculty in Paris. Allegedly fearing a right wing attack by neo Fascists upon the left wing demonstration, the Rector of the Sorbonne calls in the police, which acts with

	extreme brutality against the demonstrators and arrests over 500 people. The Sorbonne courtyard is finally cleared by the police, which provokes further fighting in the streets of the Latin Quarter.
	The Sorbonne is closed. A student strike is called by the National Student Union of France (UNEF).
May 4, 1968	Fourteen of the arrested students are tried and given heavy sentences. The UNEF student strike is declared illegal.
May 6, 1968	A large demonstration organized by UNEF in the Latin Quarter is met with harshly repressive police action, which in turn provokes guerrilla warfare using paving stones and overturned vehicles in the Latin Quarter. Over 700 persons are treated for injuries and new arrests are made.

May 7, 1968	Students and teachers estimated at between 25 to 50 thousand march in the streets of Paris protesting police brutality, police occupation of the Sorbonne, and the harsh sentences given to the arrestees.
May 10-11, 1968	Confrontations between police and protesters reach a crescendo. Police use gas grenades, including allegedly toxic chlorides and bromides, percussion grenades, and arms. Students raise barricades, fight with paving stones, and Molotov cocktails. Fighting in the Latin Quarter goes on through the day, all night and into the dawn.
May 11, 1968	Major unions call for a general strike to oppose the police brutality against the demonstrators and bystanders. Public opinion rises strongly in favor of the students and against the government. The government grants amnesty to the arrested students and

	withdraws police from faculties. Students begin occupying the faculties that are relinquished by the police.
May 13, 1968	A massive one day general strike and a demonstration of students, workers, unions, left wing political figures, teachers and others files through the streets of Paris, reportedly a million strong.
May 14, 1968	Workers spontaneously go on strike at the Sud Aviation plant in Nantes and occupy the facility
May 14, 1968	The Renault plant at Cleon goes on strike.
May 15, 1968	The Renault plants at Flins and le Mans go on strike.
May 16, 1968	The Renault plant at Billancourt outside of Paris goes on strike.
May 17, 1968	The Peugot factory goes on strike outside of Paris. Wildcat strikes spread spontaneously. Public sector utility and postal

	workers go on strike.
May 20, 1968	Wildcat strikes have spread throughout the country. An estimated ten million workers or 2/3 of the workforce is on strike.
May 23, 1968	Unions and the government engage in substantial trade union negotiations. Protesters attack police headquarters in the center of Paris.
May 24, 1968	The stock exchange is set on fire, allegedly by left wing protesters. De Gaulle promises University reforms and a plebiscite on "greater participation" in French institutions by the populace. An attempt to reform the economy through an omnibus wages agreement with the unions called the Grenelle Accords is announced.
May 25-27, 1968	The Grenelle Accords are concluded but rejected by the union rank and file.
May 29, 1968	With calls for his resignation

	and a left-wing popular front movement coalescing, De Gaulle mysteriously disappears. He removes personal papers from the Elysee Palace, tells Pompidou "he is the future" but secretly goes to Baden-Baden in Germany to seek the support of right wing French military leaders.
May 30-31, 1968	De Gaulle returns from Germany with pledges of French military support. He allows rumors of his impending resignation to fester, generating fears of impending chaos. A Communist led demonstration of upwards of 500,000 marches through the streets to taunt De Gaulle with chants of "goodbye", then De Gaulle announces on the radio that the "greater participation" plebiscite is canceled, the National Assembly will be dissolved, and there will be June general elections. He will not resign. He threatens

	assumption of extraordinary Presidential powers under the Constitution if disorder continues, and orders workers to return to work, which is viewed by the unions as a serious threat to the rank and file. A right wing demonstration of 800,000 takes to the streets in support of De Gaulle. The Communist party and union do not oppose De Gaulle. A feared occupation of governmental buildings by leftists does not occur.
June 16, 1968	Police retake the Sorbonne and other Paris faculties.
June 23-30, 1968	De Gaulle's party wins the general elections handily.

Lightning Source UK Ltd.
Milton Keynes UK
UKHW02f2143290818
328006UK00014B/1593/P